T3-BRL-625

Laurie Blum's FREE MONEY Series

<u>Childcare/Education</u>

FREE MONEY FOR DAY CARE

FREE MONEY FOR PRIVATE SCHOOLS

FREE MONEY FOR COLLEGE

FREE MONEY FOR FOREIGN STUDY

<u>Health Care</u>

FREE MONEY FOR HEART DISEASE AND CANCER CARE

FREE MONEY FOR DISEASES OF AGING

FREE MONEY FOR CHILDHOOD BEHAVIORAL AND GENETIC DISORDERS

FREE MONEY FOR CHILDREN'S MEDICAL AND DENTAL CARE

FREE MONEY FOR TREATING INFERTILITY

FREE MONEY FOR TREATING EMOTIONAL AND MENTAL DISORDERS

<u>The Arts</u>

FREE MONEY FOR PEOPLE IN THE ARTS

<u>Business</u>

FREE MONEY FOR SMALL BUSINESSES & ENTREPRENEURS

HOW TO INVEST IN REAL ESTATE USING FREE MONEY

<u>Other</u>

FREE DOLLARS FROM THE FEDERAL GOVERNMENT

<u>1992-1993 Forthcoming Titles/Health (Simon & Schuster)</u>

THE COMPLETE GUIDE TO GETTING A GRANT

Laurie Blum's

FREE MONEY

for
Treating
Emotional and
Mental Disorders

A Fireside Book
Published by Simon & Schuster
New York London Toronto Sydney Tokyo Singapore

HUM REF
RC480.5
.B595
1992

FIRESIDE
Simon & Schuster Building
Rockefeller Center
1230 Avenue of the Americas
New York, New York 10020

Copyright ©1992 by Laurie Blum

All rights reserved
including the right of reproduction
in whole or in part in any form.

FIRESIDE and colophon are registered trademarks
of Simon & Schuster Inc.

Designed by Christina M. Riley
Manufactured in the United States of America

10 9 8 7 6 5 4 3 2 1

Library of Congress Cataloging-in-Publication Data is available.

ISBN: 0-671-74597-2

· · · · · · · · · · · · · · · · · · · ·

I would like to briefly but sincerely thank my "A Team," Christina Riley and Fori Kay, as well as my wonderful editor Ed Walters.

Contents

• • • • • • • • • • • • • • • • • •

Foreword

· · · · · · · · · · · · · · · · · · ·

by Elsa P. Pauley, Ph.D.
Clinical Psychologist

I can't think of any area where Laurie Blum's *Free Money*
series is more needed than in mental health. In the twelve
years that I have been in private practice, I have seen
access to both public and private funds and insurance
coverage shrink dramatically.

There are at least three areas where the average person
might be confronted with the need for treatment of a
mental or emotional disorder. First, and most seriously,
there are the cases of the chronically mentally ill, particularly those who are schizophrenic. Second, someone may
suffer from a substance abuse problem or alcoholism that
demands treatment. Third, individuals often experience
emotional problems of a more short-term nature, such as
depression and anxiety, that arise out of the situations of
everyday living. In all three instances, treatment can provide
help — hospitalization, medication, psychotherapy. But
treatment is expensive, and funding from insurance or the
government is severely limited and often hard to obtain.

Chronic mental illness is debilitating on everyone involved,
for the family as well as for the person who is ill. Long-
term maintenance in a treatment facility is very expensive.
To qualify for government assistance, the family's funds
must often be depleted, leaving the whole family as a
victim. Even if the government will assist, state and county
budgets for mental health have been cut so drastically that
there is often no care available. There are months-long

waiting lists before appointments can be given at an outpatient clinic. The public hospitals often admit only the most disturbed and dangerous patients. Even when these patients are admitted, treatment is often only medication and sedation. Ongoing care is almost unheard of. Outpatient psychotherapy is nearly impossible to obtain.

As we all know, addictions have become an increasingly disturbing problem in the United States. Alcoholism, drug abuse, eating disorders — we may be addicted ourselves; we certainly know someone who is. The most successful treatment for a problem of addiction begins in an inpatient facility for a period of approximately one month, so that detoxification can be completed, intensive counseling and introduction to 12-step programs can begin. But such facilities charge thousands of dollars for such a treatment program. Will insurance cover this? What of the income lost while treatment takes place? How are we to pay?

Most of us, at some time in our lives, experience depression or anxiety. During this recession, we may have lost our jobs. We may be going through a divorce. A parent or a child may have died. When this happens, we're confused and don't know what to do. We don't know how to handle the situation. Counseling would be appropriate, but, again, how are we to pay?

Perhaps we have insurance. Most people believe that private insurance covers mental and emotional disorders in the same way that medical problems are covered. Unfortunately, that is not generally the case. Insurance companies typically limit how much they will spend for hospitalization. Medication which is needed to stabilize long-term conditions such as manic-depression may not be covered by insurance, or may be covered only partially. Reimbursement for outpatient psychotherapy has strict limitations. There may be a high deductible; the number of counseling visits may be limited; there may be a maximum benefit per visit. The remaining cost is left to us or our family.

Unfortunately, the time when people seem to need psychotherapy the most tends to be when they can afford it the least. In these recessionary times, counseling is often a luxury and just has to be put off, even though it could be of enormous benefit. It is terribly sad to me when someone who desperately needs counseling must stop because he/ she cannot continue to pay for it. While I always try, in my private practice, to help people in these situations, sometimes it just isn't possible. Where can people turn?

Laurie Blum provides indispensable assistance to those who may not be able to afford treatment for a mental or emotional problem. She provides sources for funding both the medical bills themselves and for recovering the loss of income which can occur when such a disorder becomes severe. She addresses the areas of both long-term care and more short-term treatment. She lists ways that the co-payment portion of medical expenses can be recovered. In such emotionally and financially precarious times, such advice may decide whether treatment can be provided or not, whether a family is further devastated or not.

We all hope that emotional problems will not happen to us or to someone in our family. But, if they do happen, we want to provide the best of care to the person in need. Laurie Blum provides options in this guide that are not widely known, but are nonetheless available to anyone. Such advice in invaluable indeed.

Introduction

· · · · · · · · · · · · · · · · · · ·

The emotional factors facing an individual undergoing treatment for an emotional or mental disorder, whether of short duration or requiring longer term care, can be difficult enough. The added burden of attempting to solve how to pay for this care can be all but overwhelming. Some 38 million Americans have no health insurance. Those who are insured often have policies that do not cover treatment for emotional or mental disorders. And when an individual is lucky enough to have a policy that does allow for payment, in most cases there are strict limitations on the number of visits and/or length of inpatient stay, as well as what can often be sizable deductible and coinsurance provisions.

The number of Americans requiring treatment is sizable. There are nine million alcoholics in the U.S.; 350,000 of them are hospitalized each year. One out of every ten Americans suffer from acute depression at some point in their lives. Three million Americans have some sort of substance abuse or dependency problem; 30,000 are hospitalized each year. Manic/depressive illness affects 750,000 Americans each year, while two million schizophrenics are diagnosed each year, some of whom require continuous institutional care.

Free Money for Treating Emotional & Mental Disorders directs readers to the hundreds of thousands of dollars available annually to help offset both medical expenses (such as doctor and hospital bills) and reimbursement for the loss of regular income. Much of the available money is awarded without regard to the financial status of the recipient and none of it ever needs to be paid back. The book includes information on funding available in all fifty states.

The book is divided into six chapters:

1. **"Associations: Funding and Referral Information"** (listing foundations and associations that provide a wide range of services, including: publishing information, sponsoring and referring patients and their families to support groups, providing physician referrals, funds for research, and patient services);

2. **"Corporate/Employee Grants"** (listing companies and corporations that provide grants for their employees or former employees);

3. **"Private Foundation Funding"** (listing sources to help individuals pay for medical treatment as a result of specific disorders or medical problems);

4. **"Flow-through Funding"** (providing information about foundation monies that are given to individuals through sponsoring organizations);

5. **"State and Regional Government Grants"** (including local and state health care offices);

6. **"Federal Grants"** (identifying agencies offering direct funding and/or essential referral information).

Where possible, listings within each chapter are arranged state-by-state to make this book as easy to use as possible. Check your state's listings in all six chapters to see which grants or corporate programs apply to you. You'll find funding parameters and an address and phone number for further information and application forms.

By the time this book is published, some of the information contained here will have changed. No reference book can be as up-to-date as the reader or the author would like. Names, addresses, dollar amounts, telephone numbers, and other data are always in flux; however, most of the information will not have changed.

While reviewing this data, readers are advised to remember that funding sources are not without restrictions and that researching, applying for, and receiving aid will take time, effort, diligence, and thought. You are going to have to identify the sources of aid for which you qualify and determine whether or not you fulfill geographic and other requirements. You are going to have to fill out applications. You may meet with rejection and frustration somewhere along this road. The odds, however, are in your favor that you will qualify for some sort of funding assistance.

On the next page is a concise how-to guide to writing a grant proposal. Follow my instructions and you should be successful in obtaining some sort of assistance. Good luck.

How to apply

As indicated by the number of listings in this book, thousands of resources for health-related funding exist throughout the country from government, private foundation, and corporate sources. Applying for this aid is the challenging part; it requires diligence, thought and organization.

First is the sorting out or research/gathering phase. Look through each chapter of the book and mark each potential assistance source. Pay close attention to the listed restrictions and qualifications, eliminating from your list the resources least likely to assist you.

Then, politely contact each of your listed sources by mail or phone to verify all current information, such as address, telephone, name of proper contact, and his/her title (in cases where the contact's name is not listed, begin your letter, "To Whom It May Concern"). At this time, you can also arrange to get a copy of the source's most current assistance guidelines, and an application form if one is required. Use this opportunity to find out about any application deadlines and to ask where you are in the funding cycle (i.e., if there is no deadline, when would be the best time to apply; also, be sure to ask when awards will be announced and funds distributed). However, do not "grill" or cross-examine the person you reach on the phone. Always be prepared to talk about why you are applying and what you are applying for — in case you ring through to the key decision maker, who decides to interview you on the spot!

Second is the application phase. Most often you will be asked to submit a formal application (rather than a proposal). Always be sure to read (and follow!) the instructions for completing the application. Usually the same material used for one application can be applied to most, if not all, of your other applications, with a little restructuring. Make sure you answer each and every question as asked, appropriate to each application.

Grant applications take time (and thought) to fill out, so make sure to give yourself enough time to thoroughly complete the application before its deadline. Filling out the application can be a lengthy process, because you may be required to write one or more essays. Often, what is required is a "statement of purpose" explaining why you need the assistance for which you are applying. You may also need time to assemble required attachments, such as tax returns and other financial records. (Don't worry, in most cases you won't be penalized for having money in the bank.) You may also be required to include personal references. Be sure to get strong references. Call all of the people you plan to list and ask them if they feel comfortable giving you references. Remember, you have to convince the grantors to give money to you and not to someone else.

Be clear, concise, and neat! You may very well write a top-notch application, but it won't look good if it's been prepared in a sloppy manner. Applications (and proposals) should always be typed and double-spaced. Make sure you keep a copy after you send off the original — I have learned the hard way that there is nothing worse than having the funding source be unable to find your application and your having to reconstruct it because you didn't keep a copy.

You should apply to a number of funding sources for grants and awards, as no one application is guaranteed to win an award. Although none of the sources listed in this book requires an application fee, the effort you will have to put in will probably limit you to a maximum of eight applications. If you are ambitious and want to apply to more than eight sources, go right ahead. Remember, the more sources you apply to, the greater your chances for success.

COMPONENTS OF
A SUCCESSFUL PROPOSAL

One of the largest categories of grants that are given to individuals are grants for general welfare and medical assistance. The various funding agencies that make these awards have happily made applying for these grants much simpler than for other categories. Most, if not all, of the foundations you will be applying to will require the following in order to consider your request for funding:

1. A brief but complete letter outlining you or your family member's medical problem and/or expenses and bills you have incurred because of this problem. In the final paragraph of your letter, you should specify a dollar amount that you feel confident would ease your financial burden (i.e., "I request a grant in the amount of $2,500 to help me pay for xyz treatment, which is not covered by my medical insurance.")

2. A report from the doctors or hospital staff involved with the patient on whose behalf the grant proposal is being submitted. Because of the enormous volume of mail that most foundations receive, you may want to get the medical reports directly from doctors and/or hospital personnel and submit them with your application. This way there is no chance that a foundation can delay or turn down your application on the grounds that it is incomplete.

3. A copy of your tax return. Do not panic! You will not be penalized for showing excellent earnings or having savings. The issue is how the costs associated with the medical problems or care needs with which you are faced alter your financial stability. However, if you are in financial need, you will certainly be given every consideration.

4. A personal interview. This may take place by phone or in person. Stay calm. Foundations are run by people committed to their mission of helping those in need or in trouble. Simply state the facts of your case and needs and all will go well.

Remember, your application should be clear and concise. Your letter should not exceed two pages. Be sure to include any attachments the foundation might require, such as medical reports and tax returns. Follow my instructions and you should qualify for some sort of "free money."

Associations:
Funding and
Referral Information

This chapter is an invaluable resource guide for the patient and his/her family. It contains listings of foundations/associations that address the needs of individuals with specific disorders or medical problems. Among the many services they provide, these organizations publish information, sponsor and refer patients and their families to support groups, give physician referrals, and award funds for research as well as for patient services. Though not all of the foundations/associations offer monies to be paid directly to patients, I felt it was imperative that I include this information in this book. The comfort and support that a professional association offers the patient and his/her family can be very important.

The chapter is organized by the type of association and/or disorder. The various foundations and associations are listed alphabetically under the names of the types of associations and/or disorders that they address.
Patients and their families will probably find that the various staff members of these foundations/associations can be exceedingly helpful during difficult times. Use them and their associations to your best advantage.

ASSOCIATIONS

. . . .

GENERAL MENTAL HEALTH ASSOCIATIONS

American Association of Orthomolecular Medicine
900 North Federal Highway
Suite 330
Boca Raton, FL 33432
(407) 393-6167

Description: Division of the Huxley Institute for Biosocial Research, made up of research scientists seeking ways to treat mental disorders by altering the brain's molecular/chemical/enzymatic environment; provides referral service
Contact: Mary Roddy Haggerty, Executive Director

American Mental Health Fund
2735 Hartland Road
Suite 302
Falls Church, VA 22043
(703) 573-2200
FAX (703) 207-9894

Description: Fundraising organization that supports research, increases public awareness, provides public education, and fights stigma associated with mental illness
Contact: James Hawkins, Chairman
Call: (800) 433-5959 to order information booklet only

Deaf-Reach
3722 12th Street, N.E.
Washington, DC 20017
(202) 832-6681

Description: Local service provider to deaf persons with mental/emotional problems; operates group homes for mentally ill deaf persons; provides referral services, housing placement assistance, personal counseling, day programs, community advocacy activities; publishes newsletter and brochure
Contact: Carole Schauer, Executive Director

Hogg Foundation for Mental Health
Box 7998
University Station
University of Texas
Austin, TX 78712
(512) 471-5041

Description: Agency funding programs in Texas; publishes several books and pamphlets on mental health, including *Mental Health in Nursing Homes, Individual Freedom and the Requirements of Modern Society, Emotional Maturity,* and *Family Violence: The Well-Kept Secret*
Contact: Publications Division

**Huxley Institute for
Biosocial Research**
900 North Federal Highway
Suite 330
Boca Raton, FL 33432
(407) 393-6167
(800) 847-3802

Description: Research and training institute concerned with mental health disorders and treatment/rehabilitation resources; offers educational services to family members, professionals, community organizations, and government agencies; maintains referral center in New York City and library on orthomolecular treatment of schizophrenia and other disorders
Contact: Mary Roddy Haggerty, Executive Director

**The Information Exchange
on Young Adult Chronic
Patients**
151 South Main Street
Suite 212
New York, NY 10956
(914) 634-0050

Description: Information clearinghouse for the professional and public exchange of data on research and treatment of 18-35 year old psychiatric patients who have required at least two years of mental health services; sponsors research, training, and community presentations; maintains library
Contact: Bert Pepper, M.D., Executive Director

**National Association for
Rural Mental Health**
12300 Twinbrook Parkway
Suite 320
Rockville, MD 20852
(301) 984-6200

Description: Fundraising and professional training organization; works to promote effective mental health services in rural areas

**National Council of
Community Mental Health
Centers**
12300 Twinbrook Parkway
Suite 320
Rockville, MD 20852
(301) 984-6200

Description: Alliance of mental health organizations and interested individuals dedicated to improving mental health services and promoting full insurance coverage for treatment; offers publications and resource materials
Contact: Charles G. Ray, Executive Director

ASSOCIATIONS

• •

Wisconsin Clearinghouse
University of Wisconsin
Hospital and Clinics
1954 East Wisconsin Avenue
Madison, WI 53704
(608) 263-2797

Description: Clearinghouse for information and materials on mental health, women's issues, alcohol and drug abuse, and youth development; offers books, reprints, pamphlets, periodicals, posters, etc.

SOCIETIES OF MENTAL HEALTH PROFESSIONALS

American Psychiatric Association
1400 K Street, N.W.
Washington, DC 20005
(202) 682-6000
FAX (202) 682-6114

Description: Professional society of physicians with specialized training in psychiatry
Contact: Melvin Sabshin, M.D., Medical Director

American Psychoanalytic Association
309 East 49th Street
New York, NY 10022
(212) 752-0450

Description: Professional organization of psychologists and psychoanalysis students at accredited schools
Contact: Helen Fischer, Administrative Director

American Psychological Association
1200 17th Street, N.W.
Washington, DC 20036
(202) 955-7600
FAX (703) 525-5191

Description: Professional/scientific society of psychologists
Contact: Raymon D. Fowler, CEO

Association for Advancement of Behavior Therapy
15 West 36th Street
New York, NY 10018
(212) 279-7970
FAX (212) 239-8038

Description: Professional organization primarily for psychologists interested in behavior modification; provides referral service and speakers' bureau
Contact: Mary Jane Eimer, CAE, Executive Director

Association for Applied Psychophysiology and Biofeedback
10200 West 44th Avenue
Suite 304
Wheat Ridge, CO 80033
(303) 422-8436
FAX (303) 422-8894

Description: Organization for mental health professionals and others interested in biofeedback
Contact: Francine Butler, Ph.D., Executive Director

Council for the National Register of Health Service Providers in Psychology
1730 Rhode Island Avenue, N.W.
Suite 1200
Washington, DC 20036
(202) 833-2377
FAX (202) 296-0831

Description: Society of psychologists who are licensed or certified by state/provincial boards of examiners of psychology
Contact: Judy E. Hall, Ph.D.

Special Interest Group on Phobias and Related Anxiety Disorders
c/o Carol Lindemann, Ph.D.
245 East 87th Street
New York, NY 10028
(212) 860-5560

Description: Professional organization for health care workers interested in the treatment of anxiety disorders
Contact: Carol Lindemann, Ph.D., Chair

ASSOCIATIONS

. . . .

FACILITIES/TREATMENT PROGRAMS

The Bridge
248 West 108th Street
New York, NY 10025
(212) 663-3000

Description: Mental health and rehabilitation facility for chronic mentally/emotionally disabled adults and for homeless mentally disabled adults; offers community residence housing, rehabilitation programs, vocational training, job placement
Contact: Murray Itzkowitz, Executive Director

Entertainment Industry Referral and Assistance Center
11132 Ventura Boulevard
Suite 410
Studio City, CA 91604
(818) 848-9997

Description: Employee assistance program for individuals in the entertainment industry; arranges substance abuse treatment (drugs/alcohol); offers counseling services in California; provides nationwide referral service
Contact: Dae Sullender-Medman, Director

Mental Research Institute (MRI)
555 Middlefield Road
Palo Alto, CA 94301
(415) 321-3055

Description: Behavioral science-oriented organization that offers professional training, research, educational programs, and workshops; operates sliding-scale free clinic for short-term, family-oriented therapy; provides emergency treatment for family violence; operates specialized clinical centers for problems such as eating disorders and depression; maintains speakers' bureau and 1500-volume library
Contact: Joyce Emamjomeh, Administrator

Occupational Program Consultants Association
c/o Kris Brennan
Lincoln EAP, Inc.
201 North 8th Street
No. 101
Lincoln, NE 68508
(402) 476-0186

Description: Consulting agency that provides employee assistance program services to businesses; helps businesses put these programs in place, so that employees with substance abuse problems and/or emotional problems can be referred for treatment
Contact: Kris Brennan, President

• • • • • • • • • • • • • • • • • •

**Social/Vocational Rehabili-
tation Clinic**
c/o Post-Graduate Center
West
344 West 36th Street
New York, NY 10018
(212) 971-3200

Description: Psychiatric outpatient clinic providing comprehensive therapeutic program with the goals of reducing
inpatient hospital admissions and promoting independent
living and social integration; offers case management
services
Contact: Michael Bellotti, Program Director

SUPPORT ORGANIZATIONS

SUPPORT ORGANIZATIONS FOR ANXIETY DISORDERS

**Anxiety Disorders Associa-
tion of America**
6000 Executive Boulevard
Suite 200
Rockville, MD 20852
(301) 231-8368

Description: 4000-member group of professionals and family
members concerned about anxiety disorders (phobias, panic
disorders, obsessive-compulsive disorders, etc.); supports
research; provides public and professional education; fosters
local self-help groups; serves as information clearinghouse
Contact: Susan Kanaan, Executive Director

Fly Without Fear
310 Madison Avenue
New York, NY 10017
(212) 697-7666

Description: For-profit local weekly support group for
individuals afraid of airline travel; conditioning exercises
include meetings with ground controllers and safety experts,
visits to airports, and "Seminar in the Sky" flights; also
provides lectures on fear of flying to other organizations
Contact: Carol Gross, Director

**Obsessive-Compulsive
Anonymous**
P.O. Box 215
New Hyde Park, NY 11040
(516) 741-4901

Description: Self-help group for individuals with obsessive-
compulsive disorders; uses 12-step recovery program;
publishes book, *Obsessive Compulsive Anonymous*
Contact: Roy C.

ASSOCIATIONS

• • • • • • • • • • • • • • • • • • •

Obsessive Compulsive Foundation
P.O. Box 9573
New Haven, CT 06535
(203) 772-0565
FAX (203) 498-8476

Description: Support organization made up of professionals, individuals with OCD, and family members; conducts research; disseminates information; offers educational programs; assists with the formation and funding of local support groups
Contact: James W. Broatch, Executive Director

PASS-Group
Panic Attack Sufferers'
Support Group
6 Mahogany Drive
Williamsville, NY 14221
(716) 689-4399

Description: Telephone counseling program for individuals experiencing panic attacks and/or agoraphobia
Contact: Shirley Swede, Program Coordinator

Phobia Clinic
White Plains Hospital Center
Davis Avenue at East Post
Road
White Plains, NY 10601
(914) 681-1038

Description: Model program (local in scope) for treating individuals with phobias through the use of "contextual therapy;" offers intensive course, self-help groups, 8-week clinics, and individual therapy
Contact: Manuel D. Zane, M.D., Director

TERRAP Programs
Territorial Apprehensiveness
Programs
648 Menlo Avenue
No. 5
Menlo Park, CA 94025
(800) 274-6242
(800) 2-PHOBIA

Description: For-profit organization providing information and counseling on the self-help treatment of anxieties, fears, and phobias, with emphasis on agoraphobia; conducts research; trains professionals in the TERRAP Method; maintains library; produces newsletter for people with phobias ($18/yr)
Contact: Arthur B. Hardy, M.D., Executive Officer

SUPPORT ORGANIZATIONS FOR BRAIN INJURY

Academy of Aphasia
c/o Dr. Audrey Holland
University of Pittsburgh
Department of
Otolaryngology
Pittsburgh, PA 15260
(412) 627-5681
FAX (412) 647-2080

Description: Society of medical specialists in the field of aphasia (defect in comprehension and/or use of language due to brain disease/injury); encourages research and interdisciplinary scientific communication
Contact: Dr. Audrey Holland, Chairperson

National Head Injury Foundation (NHIF)
333 Turnpike Road
Southborough, MA 01772
(508) 485-9950
(800) 444-NHIF information service
FAX (508) 488-9893

Description: National association providing supportive services and information to head injury survivors and their families; serves as information clearinghouse on head injury and its rehabilitation; maintains support group network; offers public education; fosters research; provides advocacy services; maintains hotline and speakers' bureau
Contact: Marilyn Price Spivack, President

SUPPORT ORGANIZATIONS FOR DEPRESSION

Depression After Delivery
P.O. Box 1282
Morrisville, PA 19067
(215) 295-3994

Description: Support organization for women who have experienced postpartum depression or psychosis, as well as for their families; serves as information clearinghouse on these issues; offers referral service, hotline, quarterly newsletter
Contact: Nancy Berchtold, Executive Director

ASSOCIATIONS

• • • • • • • • • • • • • • • • • •

Depressives Anonymous:
Recovery from Depression
329 East 62nd Street
New York, NY 10021
(212) 689-2600

Description: 3000-member self-help organization for individuals experiencing depression or anxiety; offers classes, weekly meetings, newsletter, brochures, and pamphlets; supports research
Contact: Dr. Helen DeRosis, Founder

Foundation for Depression
and Manic Depression
7 East 67th Street
New York, NY 10021
(212) 772-3400

Description: Research and training institution sponsoring clinical drug trial program for patients unresponsive to currently available medications; conducts cocaine/substance abuse treatment program; has psycho-diagnostic laboratory on site
Contact: Ronald R. Fieve, M.D., President

National Depressive and
Manic Depressive Assn.
53 West Jackson Boulevard
Suite 505
Chicago, IL 60604
(312) 939-2442
FAX (312) 939-1241

Description: 30,000-member support and advocacy organization made up of depressive and manic depressive individuals and their families; promotes research; sponsors lectures; conducts confidential local meetings; provides telephone information and support service
Contact: Susan Dime-Meenan, Executive Director

National Foundation for
Depressive Illness
P.O. Box 2257
New York, NY 10116
(212) 620-7637
(800) 248-4344

Description: Organization of professionals and patients interested in affective mood disorders; provides information; offers education programs to professionals and the public; maintains speakers' bureau and referral service
Contact: Peter Ross, Executive Director

Postpartum Support, International
927 North Kellogg Avenue
Santa Barbara, CA 93111
(805) 967-7636

Description: Support network encouraging research, promoting public awareness, and supporting the formation of peer support groups dealing with the mental health issues of childbearing; addresses legal and insurance coverage issues; offers educational programs and newsletter
Contact: Jane Honikman, President

SUPPORT ORGANIZATIONS FOR EATING DISORDERS

American Anorexia/Bulimia Association
418 East 76th Street
New York, NY 10021
(212) 734-1114

Description: Information and referral resource for anorectics, bulimics, family members, and professionals; offers counseling, speakers' bureau, library, newsletter, telephone referral service; supports self-help groups
Contact: Randi Wirth, Ph.D., Executive Director

ANAD
National Association of Anorexia Nervosa and Associated Disorders
Box 7
Highland Park, IL 60035
(708) 831-3438

Description: Resource center for information about eating disorders; offers advocacy services (against insurance discrimination, dangerous diet aids), speakers' bureau, referral services, education and early detection programs, library; organizes self-help groups; promotes research
Contact: Vivian Meehan, Executive Director

Anorexia Nervosa and Related Eating Disorders
P.O. Box 5102
Eugene, OR 97405
(503) 344-1144

Description: Information clearinghouse and professional training center for treatment of anorexia nervosa, bulimia, and other eating disorders; provides referral service, support groups, counseling, and public educational presentations; affiliated with comprehensive eating disorders treatment program at Sacred Heart Hospital in Eugene, Oregon
Contact: Dr. J. Bradley Rubel, President

ASSOCIATIONS

• • • • • • • • • • • • • • • • • • •

National Anorexic Aid Society
1925 East Dublin
Granville Road
Columbus, OH 43229
(614) 436-1112

Description: Organization composed of anorectics, family members, and health care professionals; provides self-help groups, community education programs, referral services, general information, and early detection guidance
Contact: Arline Iannicello, Program Director

SUPPORT ORGANIZATIONS FOR SCHIZOPHRENIA

American Schizophrenia Association
900 North Federal Highway
Suite 330
Boca Raton, FL 33432
(407) 393-6167

Description: Organization composed of health care professionals, patients, and family members; promotes research into biochemical and genetic causes of schizophrenia; advocates improved treatment; provides public and professional education; offers referral service for the orthomolecular treatment of mental illness; publishes brochure
Contact: Mary Roddy Haggerty, Executive Director

Schizophrenics Anonymous
1209 California Road
Eastchester, NY 10709
(914) 337-2252

Description: Self-help organization sponsored by the American Schizophrenia Association; offers 12-step recovery program for diagnosed schizophrenics with discussion topics including symptoms/treatment, responsibility, and associated guilt; provides newsletter and health information
Contact: Elizabeth A. Plante, Director

SUPPORT ORGANIZATIONS FOR STRESS

American Institute of Stress
124 Park Avenue
Yonkers, NY 10703
(914) 963-1200
FAX (914) 965-6267

Description: Information clearinghouse on personal and social consequences of stress; compiles research data; evaluates stress management programs; sponsors symposia, workshops, and consulting services
Contact: Paul J. Rosch, M.D., President and Chairman

• • • • • • • • • • • • • • • • • •

Institute for the Development of Emotional and Life Skills (IDEALS)
P.O. Box 391
State College, PA 16804
(814) 237-4805

Description: Training center for the improvement of emotional and interpersonal skills, on both the professional mental health worker's level and on the ordinary worker/manager's level; promotes reduced stress in family and business environments
Contact: Joyce Fonash, Executive Director

Institute for Labor and Mental Health
3137 Telegraph Avenue
Oakland, CA 94609
(415) 653-6166

Description: Agency dealing with issues of occupational stress; identifies causes; promotes communication; assists unions with grievances; provides counseling; offers legal advocacy services; advises government and businesses on stress reduction
Contact: Dr. Richard Epstein, Director

International Association for Clear Thinking
3939 West Spencer Street
P.O. Box 1011
Appleton, WI 54912
(414) 739-8311

Description: Center providing services to individuals who want to reduce the level of emotional stress in their lives; teaches Rational Behavior Therapy coping skills; offers self-help programs, individualized support, seminars, workshops, counseling sessions, support groups, and literature
Contact: Shirley Bender, Executive Director

Society for Traumatic Stress Studies
435 North Michigan Avenue
Suite 1717
Chicago, IL 60611
(312) 644-0828
FAX (312) 644-8557

Description: Research organization studying the treatment of individuals with traumatic stress disorders; provides information, seminars, and lawyer referral service
Contact: Robert Tonai, Executive Officer

ASSOCIATIONS

• • • • • • • • • • • • • • • • •

MISCELLANEOUS SUPPORT ORGANIZATIONS

Emotional Health Anonymous
2420 San Gabriel Boulevard
Rosemead, CA 91770
(818) 573-5482

Description: Self-help group for individuals recovering from emotional problems and emotional illnesses; offers crisis intervention services; sponsors daily meetings in southern California; publishes newsletter, pamphlets, etc.
Contact: Mary Thomas, Office Manager

Emotions Anonymous
P.O. Box 4245
St. Paul, MN 55104
(612) 647-9712
FAX (612) 647-1593

Description: Self-help organization serving individuals with emotional illnesses; provides literature and information; makes telephone referrals to local chapters
Contact: William Roath, Coordinator

Molesters Anonymous (M.AN)
c/o Batterers Anonymous
1269 North E Street
San Bernardino, CA 92405
(714) 355-1100

Description: Self-help group for child molesters
Contact: Jerry M. Coffman, Ph.D., Coordinator

National Mental Health Consumer Self-Help Clearinghouse
311 South Juniper Street
Room 902
Philadelphia, PA 19107
(215) 735-6367

Description: Organization providing technical assistance to people attempting to develop self-help projects for mental health issues; provides informational referrals, written materials, and consultations
Contact: Paolo del Vecchio, Coordinator

• • • • • • • • • • • • • • • • • • •

National Self-Help Clearing-house
25 West 43rd Street
Room 620
New York, NY 10036
(212) 642-2944

Description: Clearinghouse for information on and referrals to self-help groups; maintains speakers' bureau and 200-volume library; supports research and training; offers newsletter and brochures
Contact: Frank Riessman, Co-Director

Neurotics Anonymous International Liaison
11140 Bainbridge Drive
Little Rock, AR 72212
(501) 221-2809

Description: 10,000-member self-help organization using a 12-step program of recovery from emotional illness; holds meetings for mentally and emotionally disturbed individuals to exchange experiences and recovery stories; publishes quarterly newsletter, pamphlets, books, etc.
Contact: Grover Boydston, Chairman

Recovery
802 North Dearborn Street
Chicago, IL 60610
(312) 337-5661

Description: Mental health organization promoting neuropsychiatrist Abraham A. Low's self-help method of controlling temperamental behavior and changing attitudes toward fears and nervous symptoms; publishes newsletter; has 1000 community-level groups
Contact: Mary Jane Maggio, Administrative Director

Self Abuse Finally Ends (SAFE)
c/o Karen Conterio
P.O. Box 267810
Chicago, IL 60626
(312) 722-3113
(800) DONTCUT information line

Description: Self-help group for self-injuring persons; maintains speakers' bureau; compiles statistics
Contact: Karen Conterio

ASSOCIATIONS

• • • • • • • • • • • • • • • • • •

Self-Help Center
1600 Dodge Avenue
Suite S-122
Evanston, IL 60201
(708) 328-0470
(800) 322-MASH

Description: Clearinghouse for information on various types of self-help groups; conducts workshops, training programs, and research on effectiveness of self-help group approach; maintains computer database; publishes brochures, pamphlets, workbooks, and directories of existing self-help groups
Contact: Daryl Isenberg, Ph.D., Executive Director

CONSUMER ADVOCACY GROUPS

National Alliance for the Mentally Ill
2101 Wilson Boulevard
Suite 302
Arlington, VA 22201
(703) 524-7600
FAX (703) 524-9094

Description: Alliance of self-help support groups and political advocacy groups concerned with the quality treatment and legal rights of individuals with severe/chronic mental illnesses; national office serves as information clearinghouse and offers referrals to local groups, which provide emotional/practical support for families and maintain libraries; provides speakers' bureau; promotes research; publishes newsletter and brochures
Contact: Laurie M. Flynn, Executive Director

National Association of Psychiatric Survivors
P.O. Box 618
Sioux Falls, SD 57101
(605) 334-4067

Description: 2000-member organization of current and former mental health patients, family members, and others interested in the rights of mental health patients; seeks to end involuntary psychiatric intervention and forced treatments in favor of self-help and peer support group approaches, and other nonmedical alternatives; fights social stigma attached to mental illness; provides referral and advocacy services, speakers' bureau, newsletter, and brochure
Contact: Rae Unzicker, Coordinator

• • • • • • • • • • • • • • • • • • • •

National Mental Health Association (NMHA)
1021 Prince Street
Alexandria, VA 22314-2971
(703) 684-7722
(800) 969-NMHA
FAX (703) 684-5968

Description: Consumer advocacy organization promoting mental health research; assesses quality of care at various mental health care facilities; serves as national clearing-house for educational materials; conducts public education campaigns
Contact: Preston J. Garrison, Executive Director

National Mental Health Consumers' Association
P.O. Box 1166
Madison, WI 53701

Description: Consumer advocacy organization composed of mental health care professionals, current and former patients, and other interested persons; actively promotes the creation of local self-help groups
Contact: Patrick Irick, Chairperson

Project Overcome
2121 16th Avenue
Suite 104
Minneapolis, MN 55404
(612) 871-7672

Description: Consumer advocacy organization made up of current and former mental health care patients; seeks to eliminate social stigma attached to mental illness; offers speakers' bureau, seminars, lectures, newsletter; maintains library
Contact: Rosalind Artison-Koenning, Executive Director

Reclamation, Inc.
2502 Waterford
San Antonio, TX 78217
(512) 824-8618

Description: Organization composed of former mental health care patients seeking to remove the stigma associated with mental illness; provides assistance in living outside the hospital setting (resocialization, employment, and housing); seeks to improve media coverage and public image of mental health patients; provides political advocacy services; maintains library and speakers' bureau; publishes quarterly newsletter
Contact: Don H. Culwell, Director

Private Foundation Funding

The listings in this chapter are probably the easiest and most accessible funding sources for the average individual seeking a grant. Until now, this information has not been readily available to the general public. And yet thousands of foundations give away millions of dollars to individuals to help them pay for medical treatment as a result of specific disorders or medical problems. In many cases, foundations also provide funding to help individuals cope with the loss of regular income that is often a devastating side-effect of such illness.

Do you just walk up, hold out your hand, and expect someone to put money in it? Of course not. Getting grant money takes time, effort, and thought on your part. You are going to have to find out who is giving away money. You are going to have to fill out applications. You may meet with frustration or rejection somewhere down the road. The odds, however, are in your favor that you will qualify for some sort of funding.

The information in this chapter is organized by state. Wherever possible, each listing includes a description of what the foundation funds, any restrictions (i.e., you must reside in a particular town or city), the total amount of money awarded annually, the number of grants or loans made annually, the range of monies given, the average size of the award, information on how to apply, deadline date(s), and the name(s) of contact person(s).

PRIVATE FOUNDATION FUNDING

• •

ALABAMA

Kate Kinloch Middleton Fund
P.O. Drawer 2527
Mobile, AL 36601
phone: N/A

Description: Grants or low interest loans to help defray the costs of unexpected serious illness.
Restrictions: Limited to residents of Mobile County, Alabama
$ Given: In FY89, 63 grants totaling $108,286 were awarded to individuals; range, $135 - $8,094
Application Information: Initial approach by interview

ARIZONA

Tuscon Community Fund
6601 E. Grant Rd.
Tucson, AZ 85715
(602) 722-1707

Description: The Arizona Medically Indigent Fund gives funding for catastrophic illness.
Restrictions: Limited to residents of Arizona.
$ Given: 30 grants to individuals totaling $50,000.
Application Information: Contact foundation for guidelines.
Deadline: N/A
Contact: Donna L. Grant, Executive Director

CALIFORNIA

William Babcock Memorial Endowment
305 San Anselmo Ave.
Ste. 219
San Anselmo, CA 94960
(415) 453-0901

Description: Grants and loans to persons burdened with exceptional medical expenses which exceed insurance coverage and fall outside the purview of other community agencies.
Restrictions: Limited to persons who have been residents of Marin County, California, for two or more years.
$ Given: In FY89, 480 grants totaling $445,170 were awarded to individuals; range, $50 - $10,000.
Application Information: Call for application guidelines; formal application required
Deadline: None
Contact: Executive Director

● ● ● ● ● ● ● ● ● ● ● ● ● ● ● ● ● ● ●

Albert B. Cutter Memorial Fund
Security Pacific National
Bank
Trust Department
P.O. Box 712
Riverside, CA 92501
(714) 781-1523
ADDITIONAL ADDRESS:
P.O. Box 3189
Terminal Annex
Los Angeles, CA 92501

Description: Limited grants to persons in extreme circumstances who are not eligible for other sources of aid
Restrictions: Applicants must have been permanent residents of Riverside, California for at least one year, and must have been referred by a local agency.
$ Given: In 1989, 26 grants totalling $6,650 were awarded to individuals; range, $22 - $550.
Application Information: Applications are accepted form local agencies; individuals are referred by these agencies; formal application required; interview or presentation required.
Deadline: None.
Contact: Executive Secretary, Trust Department

Hattie Givens Testamentary Trust
1017 West 18th St.
Merced, CA 95340
APPLICATION ADDRESS
1810 M. St.
Merced, CA 95340
(209) 722-7429

Description: Grants for health care, including medical assistance.
restrictions: Intended primarily for California residents
$ Given: 3 grants for individuals totaling $9,150; range, $650 - $5,000.
Application Information: Application form required.
Deadline: None
Contact: The Trustees

Jefferson (John Percival and Mary C.) Endowment Fund
114 E. De La Guearra
Santa Barbara, CA 93102
(805) 963-8822

Description: Emergency relief assistance for medical, dental and living expenses
Restrictions: Limited to residents of Santa Barbara County, California
$ Given: In FY89, 30 grants totalling $63,000 were awarded to individuals; range, $100 - $6,500
Application Information: Initial contact by letter; formal application required
Deadline: N/A

PRIVATE FOUNDATION FUNDING

• • • • • • • • • • • • • • • • • • • •

Virginia Scatena Memorial Fund for San Francisco School Teacher
c/o Bank of America, N.A.
555 California St., 17th Fl.
San Francisco, CA 94104
phone: N/A

Description: Financial assistance to retired San Francisco school teachers who are needy, sick or disabled.
Restrictions: Limited to retired teachers of the San Francisco Public School Department
$ Given: Total grants range from $125 - $400.
Application Information: Formal application required
Deadline: None; applications reviewed semi-annually by advisory committee
Contact: Susan Morales

Sequoia Trust Fund
555 California St., 36th Fl.
San Francisco, CA 94104
(415) 393-8552

Description: Financial assistance "to needy people who, by their special talents, have given great pleasure to others."
$ Given: In FY89, two grants totaling $4,400 were awarded to individuals; range, $2000 - $2,400
Application Information: Initial contact by letter; formal application required
Deadline: None
Contact: Walter M. Baird, Secretary

COLORADO

Curtis (Effle H. and Edward H.) Trust Fund
c/o United Bank of Fort Collins, N.A.
P.O. Box 2203
Fort Collins, CO 80522
(303) 482-1100

Description: Grants for emergency medical assistance paid directly to hospitals and other medical institutions to benefit grant recipients.
Restrictions: Limited to permanent residents of Larimer County, Colorado who are under 18 years old.
$ Given: In 1989, 46 grants totaling $40,000 were awarded to individuals; range, $15 - $3,000
Application Information: Formal application required, including letter from attending physician; include copy of tax return.
Deadline: 15th of each month.
Contact: Kelly Wiedeman

Presbyterian/St. Luke's Community Foundation
55 Madison, Ste. 655
Denver, CO 80206
(303) 322-3515
FAX: (303) 322-4576

Description: Funding includes health care of elderly, women and children.
Restrictions: Limited to Colorado and Rocky Mountain region
$ Given: 4 grants to individuals totaling $200,199; range $7,320 - $96,876.
Application Information: N/A
Contact: Nancy H. Shanks, Ph.D, Executive Director

CONNECTICUT

Blue Horizon Health & Welfare Trust
c/o Reid & Riege
Lakeville, CT 06039
(203) 435-9251

Description: Financial assistance for medical costs
Restrictions: Limited to residents of Connecticut
$ Given: Grant awards range from $25 - 500.
Application Information: Initial contact by letter
Deadline: None
Contact: Frances M. Wagner, Trustee

Bridgeport Ladies Charitable Trust
c/o Citytrust
961 Main St.
Bridgeport, CT 06604
phone: N/A

Description: Funding includes health and family services
Restrictions: Intended primarily for the greater Bridgeport, CT area
$ Given: 100 grants to individuals totaling $36,305; range, $50 - $1,000.
Application Information: Applicant referred from Emily Woodside Services or community agencies
Deadlines: None
Contact: Mrs. Jeffrey S. Lockhart, President

Marion Isabelle Coe Fund
c/o Colonial Bank and Trust Company
P.O. Box 2210
Waterbury, CT 06722
phone: N/A

Description: Relief assistance to adults for general living and medical expenses. Grants provide continuing assistance to needy individuals to enable them to remain in their own homes. Awards paid in monthly installments, and are renewed annually.
Restrictions: Limited to residents of Goshen, Litchfield, Morris, and Warren, connecticut
$ Given: Monthly awards range from $45 to $140.
Application Information: Initial contact by letter
Deadline: None
Contact: Mrs. Speers

23

PRIVATE FOUNDATION FUNDING

• • • • • • • • • • • • • • • • • • • •

James Crocker Testamentary Trust
P.O. Box 1045
Canaan, CT 06108
phone: N/A

Description: Temporary assistance to individuals in extreme financial difficulty
Restrictions: Limited to residents of Winchester, Connecticut
$ Given: Grants range from $100 - $500.
Application Information: Most applications are unsolicited and not preselected. Applicants are typically referred to the Funds Manager by local clergy of all denominations. Information concerning immediate financial need required.
Deadline: N/A
Contact: Kevin F. Nelligan

The de Kay Foundation
c/o Manufacturers Hanover
Trust Company
270 Park Avenue
New York, NY 10017
(212) 270-6000

Description: Grants to elderly individuals in financial need, particularly to those who are sick or disabled or who lack proper care.
Restrictions: Limited to residents of New York, New Jersey and Connecticut
$ Given: In FY89, 83 grants totaling $202,540 were awarded to individuals; range, $350 - $7,150; general range, $1,000 - $5,000
Application Information: Initial approach by letter; formal application required.
Deadline: None
Contact: Lloyd Saltus II, Vice President

St. Luke's Nurses Benefit Fund
47 Phillips Lane
Darien, CT 06820
Phone: N/A

Description: Grants for needy graduates of St. Luke's School of Nursing
Restrictions: Limited to St. Luke's alumnae
$ Given: In FY89, one grant for $2,000 was awarded.
Application Information: Formal application required.
Deadline: None
Contact: Martha Kirk, Trustee

The Westport-Weston Foundation
c/o The Westport Bank &
Trust Company
P.O. Box 5177
Westport, CT 06881
(203) 222-6911

Description: Grants for medical and basic living expenses
Restrictions: Limited to residents of Westport and Weston, Connecticut
$ Given: Grants range from $50 - $400.
Application information: Initial contact by letter
Deadline: N/A
Contact: Susanne M. Allen, Trust Officer

● ●

Widow's Society
20 Bayberry Lane
Avon, CT 06001
(203) 678-9660

Description: financial assistance to needy women
Restrictions: Limited to residents of Connecticut
$ Given: In FY89, 118 grants totaling $122,8224 were awarded to individuals; range, $75 - $4,800.
Application Information: Applications are typically referred through social service agencies, but individuals may also submit letters
Deadline: N/A
Contact: Dorothy Johnson, President

DELAWARE

**Delaware Foundation -
Quigly Trust**
P.O. Box 1669
Wilmington, DE 19899
phone: N/A

Description: Grants for medication and medical care.
Restrictions: Limited to residents of Delaware
$ Given: Grants range from $50 - $1,500
Application Information: Formal application require; request application form from the foundation
Deadline: None
Contact: N/A

FLORIDA

**Hamilton M. & Blance C.
Forman Christian Foundation**
1850 Eller Dr., Ste. 503
Fort Lauderdale, FL 33316
phone: N/A

Description: Funding includes health services, education and youth
Restrictions: Intended primarily for Florida residents
$ Given: 2 grants to individuals totaling $4,022; range $800 - $3,222
Application Information: N/A
Deadline: N/A
Contact: Hamilton C. Forman, President

PRIVATE FOUNDATION FUNDING

• • • • • • • • • • • • • • • • • • • •

Gore Family Foundation
501 E. Las Olas
Fort Lauderdale, FL 33302
phone: N/A

Description: One-time and short term assistance grants for medical expenses, equipment for the handicapped and housing and transportation costs.
Restrictions: Limited to residents of Broward County, Florida, and surrounding areas.
$ Given: In FY89, 390 relief assistance grants totaling $279,250 were awarded to individuals.
Application Information: Write for application guidelines.
Deadline: None
Contact: N/A

Hope Foundation
2335 Tamiami Trail, North,
Ste. 510
Naples, FL 33940
(813) 262-2131

Description: Funding includes mental health, education and general charitable giving.
$ Given: 38 grants to individuals totaling $49, 983; range, $100 - $10,000.
Application Information: Initial approach by letter
Deadline: None
Contact: Philip M. Francoeur, Trustee

The Ryan Foundation
1511 W. Broadway
Oviedo, FL 32765
(407) 365-8390

Description: Emergency assistance for basic necessities including essential medical care.
Restrictions: Limited to needy local area residents in Florida.
$ Given: 77 grants to individuals totaling $62,203; range $13 - $39,704
Application Information: Initial approach by letter or telephone; application form required.
Deadline: None
Contact: Jean Beede

Roy M. Speer Foundation
1803 U.S. Highway 19
Holiday, FL 34691-5536
phone: N/A

Description: Grants to individuals in financial difficulty as a result of medical problems.
Restrictions: Limited to residents of Florida.
$ Given: One grant for $4,000 is awarded.
Application Information: Initial approach by letter.
Deadline: None
Contact: N/A

Winter Haven Hospital Charity Fund
c/o NCNB National Bank
P.O. Box 199
Orlando, FL 32802
phone: N/A

Description: Grants for medical assistance for the financially distressed
Restrictions: Limited to residents of Winter Haven, Florida
$ Given: In FY89, two grants were awarded to individuals; range, $250 - $1,500
Application Information: Write for guidelines.
Deadline: None
Contact: N/A

GEORGIA

Baker (Clark and Ruby) Foundation
c/o Bank South
Personal Trust Department,
P.O. Box 4956 (MC45)
Atlanta, GA 30302-9824
(404) 529-4627

Description: Grants primarily to retired Methodist ministers for pensions and medical assistance.
Restrictions: Residents of Georgia.
$ Given: 10 grants totaling $15,500 are awarded to individuals.
Application Information: Initial approach by letter or phone; interviews required.
Deadline: None
Contact: Richard L. Watton, Trust Officer

Thomas C. Burke Foundation
182 Riley Avenue, No. B
Macon, GA 31204-2345
(912) 745-1442

Description: Medical assistance in one of three forms: (1) one-time payments for doctor bills, medical equipment and pharmacy bills; (2) weekly grants of up to $60 to assist with medical expenses; or (3) grants for transportation to medical facilities.
Restrictions: Limited to residents of Bibb County, Georgia.
$ Given: In FY89, an unspecified number of grants totaling $120, 772 were awarded to individuals.
Deadline: None.
Contact: Carolyn P. Griggers

PRIVATE FOUNDATION FUNDING

• • • • • • • • • • • • • • • • • • • •

HAWAII

The Hawaii Community Foundation
222 Merchant St.
Honolulu, HI 96813
(808) 537-6333

Program: Winifred D. Robertson Fund
Description: One-time assistance to adult residents of Oahu, Hawaii

Program: Alice M.G. Soper Fund
Description: One-time grants to adults, age 50 or older in financial need due to illness or disability.

Program: Gwenfried Allen Fund
Description: Financial assistance for the elderly and mentally ill

Program: Irving L. Singer Funds
Description: One-time assistance to children of Hawaiian ancestry whose families are unable to pay for medical expenses, or for special education, social services, or mental health services.

Program: The Kitaro Watanabe Fund
Description: Individual assistance to children in need

Restrictions (for all programs): Limited to residents of Hawaii
$ Given: In 1989, 116 grants totalling $78,111 were awarded to individuals; range, $80 - $1,500; general range, $100 - $1,000; average, $680
Application Information: Call for application guidelines; formal application required.
Deadline: None
Contact: Suzanne Togucyi, Program Officer

The May Templeton Hopper Foundation
1412 Whitney St.
Honolulu, HI 96822
(808) 944-2807

Description: Assistance to cover costs of medication, rent, day care and other services.
Restrictions: Limited to those 62 years or older who have lived in Hawaii at least 5 years.
$ Given: 287 grants to individuals totaling $473,988; range $360 - $9,600.
Application Information: Initial approach by telephone; Formal application required.
Deadline: The fifth working day of the month to be considered that month.
Contact: Diana H. Lord, President

ILLINOIS

Reade Industrial Fund
c/o Harris Trust and Savings
Bank
P.O. Box 755
111 West Monroe Street
Chicago, IL 60690
(312) 461-7550

Description: Emergency loans or grants to individuals who are unable to care for themselves and/or their family members.
Restrictions: Limited to individual who are currently or who have previously been employed in industry in Illinois.
$ Given: Grants range from $373 - $5,000.
Application Information: Initial approach by letter; formal application required
Deadline: None
Contact: Tony Abiera

Swiss Benevolent Society of Chicago
P.O. Box 2137
Chicago, IL 60690
phone: N/A

Description: Grants to elderly and other individuals of Swiss descent or nationality in cases of need or emergency.
Restrictions: Limited to Chicago area residents of Swiss descent or nationality
$ Given: 55 grants totalling $53,450 area awarded to individuals.
Application Information: Formal application required; write for program information and current program deadlines.
Deadline: Varies.
Contact: Admiral Alan Weber, President.

INDIANA

Allen & Rose Mills Trust
c/o Irwin Union Bank &
Trust Co.
500 Washington St.
Columbus, IN 47201
phone: N/A

Description: Assistance to residents of Bartholomew County, IN with mental problems; also for needy children.
Restrictions: See above.
Application Information: N/A
Deadline: None
Contact: Stephen Kirts

Frank L. and Laura L. Smock Foundation
c/o Lincoln National Bank
and Trust Company
P.O. Box 960
Fort Wayne, IN 46801-0960
(219) 461-6477

Description: Medical assistance and nursing care to the ill, needy, disabled, blind and aged.
Restrictions: Limited to individuals of the Presbyterian faith throughout Indiana
$ Given: 33 grants to individuals totalling $148,804; range, $108 - $24,783.
Application Information: N/A
Deadline: N/A
Contact: Alice Kopfer, Assistant Vice-President

PRIVATE FOUNDATION FUNDING

• • • • • • • • • • • • • • • • • • • •

KANSAS

Charlotte Hill Charitable Trust
P.O. Box 754
Winfield, KS 67156
(316) 221-4600

Description: Grants to single women over age 60 with limited income and assets.
Restrictions: Limited to residents of the Arkansas City and Winfield, Kansas, areas
$ Given: In FY89, 62 grants totalling $75,700 were awarded to individuals; range, $40 - $5,900
Application Information: Formal application required.
Deadline: None.
Contact: Loyette Olson

Jones (Walter S. and Evan C.) Foundation
527 Commercial Street, Rm. 515
Emporia, KS 66801
(316) 342-1714
ADDITIONAL ADDRESS:
c/o Bank IV Emporia
Emporia, KS 66801

Description: Financial assistance for medical expenses. Grants based on demonstrated financial need.
Restrictions: Applicants must have been continuous residents of Lyon, Coffey or Osage counties, Kansas, for at least one year; applicants must be under 21 years of age.
$ Given: In FY89, 2,192 medical assistance grants totaling $625,074 were awarded individuals; range, $60 - $6,173.
Application Information: Initial approach by letter; formal application required; interviews required; parents of applicant must submit comprehensive financial statement.
Deadline: Prior to beginning of medical services.
Contact: Sharon R. Brown, General Manager

KENTUCKY

Al. J. Schneider Foundation Corporation
3720 Seventh St. Rd.
Louisville, KY 40216
phone: N/A

Description: Funding for Baptists Church, religious organizations, health, education and youth agencies.
Restrictions: Intended primarily for Kentucky residents
$ Given: 12 grants for individuals totaling $5,900; range, $200 - $1,000
Application Information: N/A
Deadline: N/A
Contact: N/A

• • • • • • • • • • • • • • • • • • • •

MAINE

Camden Home for Senior Citizens
66 Washington St.
Camden, ME 04843
(207) 236-2087
APPLICATION ADDRESS:
Belfast Road, Camden, ME
04843, (207) 236-2014

Description: Grants for medical care and drugs.
Restrictions: Limited to residents of Camden, Rockport, Lincolnville, and Hope, Maine.
$ Given: In FY89, 200 grants totaling $42,350 were awarded to individuals; range, $50 - $300.
Application Information: Write or call for guidelines.
Deadline: None.
Contact: Charles Lowe, President

Anita Card Montgomery Foundation
20 Mechanic Street
Camden, ME 04843-1707
phone: N/A

Description: Grants to needy individuals, including funding for medical and dental expenses.
Restrictions: Limited to residents of Camden, Rockport, Lincolnville and Hope, Maine
$ Given: Grants range from $40 -$4,060.
Application Information: Write for guidelines.
Deadline: None.
Contact: Robert C. Perkins

Portland Female Charitable Society
c/o Janet Matty
20 Noyes Street
Portland, ME 04103
phone: N/a
APPLICATION ADDRESS:
142 Pleasant Street
No. 761
Portland, ME 04101

Description: Financial aid for medical and dental expenses for children, as well as for the elderly.
Restrictions: Limited to residents of Portland, Maine
$ Given: In FY89, 33 grants totaling $9,550 were awarded; range, $20 - $850
Application Information: Write for information; applications are usually presented by health care professionals or social workers; interviews required
Deadline: None
Contact: Janet Matty

Herbert E. Wadsworth Trust
c/o Fleet Bank of Maine
Merrill Center
Exchange Street
Bangor, ME 04401
phone: N/A

Description: Financial assistance for citizens of Winthrop, Maine, who are hospitalized in a well-regulated and recognized facility outside the town of Winthrop
Restrictions: Limited to citizens of Winthrop, Maine
$ Given: In FY89, nine grants totaling $8,440 were awarded to individuals; range, $100, $3,150
Application Information: Write for guidelines.
Deadline: None.
Contact: N/A

PRIVATE FOUNDATION FUNDING

. . . .

MARYLAND

**Anna Emory Warfield
Memorial Fund, Inc.**
103 West Monument St.
Baltimore, MD 21201
(301) 547-0612

Description: Relief assistance to elderly women in the Baltimore, Maryland area
Restrictions: Limited to women in the Baltimore, Maryland area
$ Given: In 1989, 42 grants totaling $150,000 were awarded to individuals: range, $900 - $3,925
Application Information: Write to request application guidelines; formal application required.
Deadline: None
Contact: Thelma K. O'Neal, Secretary

Steeplechase Fund
400 Fair Hill Dr.
Elkton, MD 21921
phone: N/A

Description: Assistance to injured jockeys, their widows and families medical and other expenses.
Restrictions: See above.
$ Given: Grants to individuals totaling $38,995.
Application Information: Initial approach by letter; include information on medical expenses and occurrence of injury.
Deadline: N/A
Contact: Charles Colgan

MASSACHUSETTS

The Pilgrim Foundation
478 Torrey St.
Brockton, MA 02401-4654
(508) 586-6100

Description: Financial assistance to families and children.
Restrictions: Limited to residents of Brockton, Massachusetts
$ Given: Welfare assistance grants totalling $7,230 are awarded to individuals.
Application Information: Formal application required.
Deadline: N/A
Contact: Executive Director

· · · · · · · · · · · · · · · · · · ·

Sailor's Snug Harbor of Boston
c/o Adams, Harkness and Hill
One Liberty Square
Boston, MA 02109
(617) 423-6688

Description: Funding for health and welfare of individuals including the aged and sailors.
Restrictions: Intended primarily for residents of Boston, MA
$ Given: Grants range from $2,000 - $50,000
Application Information: Initial approach by proposal
Deadline: In by dates of board meetings, November 15, 1February 15, and April 15.
Contact: Stephen Little, President

Salem Female Charitable Society
175 Federal St.
Boston, MA 02110
phone: NA
APPLICATION ADDRESS:
30 Chestnut Street
Salem, MA 01970

Description: Grants to needy women of the Salem Massachusetts, area
Restrictions: Original grant limited to residents of the Salem Massachusetts, area. Recipients may, however, relocate without forfeiting grant.
$ Given: In FY89, 18 grants totaling $19,810 were awarded to individuals; range, $200 - $1,700 average, $800.
Application Information: Write for guidelines.
Deadline: None
Contact: Jane A. Phillips, Treasurer

Shaw Fund for Mariners' Children
c/o Russell Brier & Company
50 Congress St., Rm. 800
Boston, MA 02109
phone: N/A
APPLICATION ADDRESS:
64 Concord Ave.
Norwood, MA 02062

Description: Grants to financially distressed mariners and their families.
Restrictions: Limited to mariners, their wives or widows, and their children: Massachusetts residents only.
$ Given: Grants totaling $114,140 are awarded to individuals
Application Information: Write for program information
Deadline: None.
Contact: Clare M. Tolias

PRIVATE FOUNDATION FUNDING

• • • • • • • • • • • • • • • • • • •

The Swasey Fund for Relief of Public School Teachers of Newburyport, Inc.
31 Milk St.
Boston, MA 02109
(508) 462-2784
APPLICATION ADDRESS:
23 Summitt Pl.
Newburyport, MA 01950

Description: Financial aid to individuals who have taught in the Newburyport, Massachusetts public school system for at least 10 years.
Restrictions: See above.
$ Given: In FY89, 21 grants totalling $66,600 were awarded to individuals; range, $100 - $10,000.
Application Information: Formal application required.
Deadline: None.
Contact: Jean MacDonald, Treasurer

Urann Foundation
P.O Box 1788
Brockton, MA 02403
(508) 588-7744

Description: Medical assistance grants for Massachusetts families engaged in cranberry farming and processing. Grants intended to assist in payment of hospital and medical bills.
Restrictions: Limited to families located in Massachusetts.
$ Given: In 1989, 22 grants totaling $44,460 were awarded individuals; 1 medical assistance grant of $680 was awarded.
Application Information: Initial contact by phone or letter
Deadline: None.
Contact: Howard Whelan, Administrator

MINNESOTA

Fanny S. Gilfilan Memorial, Inc.
c/o Lawrence Harder, Rte. 4
Redwood Falls, MN 56283
APPLICATION ADDRESS
Redwood County Welfare
Dept., Box 27
Redwood Falls, MN 56283
(507) 637-5741

Description: Financial assistance to needy residents of Redwood County, MN including hospitalization bills.
Restrictions: See above.
Application Information: Formal application required; interviews required.
Deadline: None
Contact: N/A

Hanna R. Kristianson Trust
P.O. Box 1011
Albert Lea, MN 56007
APPLICATION ADDRESS:
Clarks Grove, MN 56016
(507) 256-4415

Description: Financial aid to needy individuals over 50 years of age.
Restrictions: Limited to residents of Freeborn County, Minnesota who are over 50 years old
$ Given: Grants range from $20 - $1,660.
Application Information: Call or write for guidelines.
Deadline: None
Contact: Richard S. Haug, Trustee

Charles D. Gilfillan Paxton Memorial, Inc.
c/o Thomas W. Murray,
Vice President
W-555 First National Bank
Building
St. Paul, MN 55101
(612) 291-6236
APPLICATION ADDRESS:
Committee of Benificiaries
200 Southwest First St.
Rochester, MN 55905
(507) 282-2511

Description: Medical assistance to financially distressed Minnesota residents; priority given to those in rural areas and towns with populations of less than 3,000
Restrictions: Limited to residents of Minnesota
$ Given: In FY89, 80 grants totalling $39,900 were awarded to individuals; range, $38 - $2,160; average, $500.
Application Information: Formal application required.
Deadline: None
Contact: Marie LaPlante, Secretary

The Saint Paul Foundation
1120 Norwest Ctr.
St. Paul, MN 55101
(612) 224-5463

Description: Relief assistance grants
Restrictions: Limited to residents of St. Paul and Minneapolis, Minnesota, and to employees of 3M Company.
$ Given: 15 relief assistance grants totalling $42,504 are awarded to individuals.
Application Information: Write or call for guidelines.
Deadline: N/A
Contact: Paul A. Verret, President

PRIVATE FOUNDATION FUNDING

• • • • • • • • • • • • • • • • • •

MISSOURI

Herschen Family Foundation
c/o Jack R. Herschen
Silver Dollar City, Inc.
Branson, MO 65616
(417) 338-2611

Description: Assistance for individuals in need.
Restrictions: Intended primarily for residents of Missouri.
$ Given: In 1989, 34 grants totaling $250,430 were awarded to individuals.
Application Information: Call or write, explaining need.
Deadline: None.
Contact: Jack R. Herschend, Director

The Leader Foundation
7711 Carondelet Ave., 10th Fl.
St. Louis, MO 63105
(314) 725-7300

Description: Funding for pensions, family services, and health organizations.
Restrictions: Intended primarily for residents of St. Louis, MO.
$ Given: 23 grants to individuals totalling $76,308; range, $600 - $6,000
Application Information: Initial approach by letter.
Deadline: None.
Contact: Edwin G. Shifrin, Vice-President

NEW HAMPSHIRE

Abble M. Griffin Hospital Fund
111 Concord St.
Nashua, NH 03060
phone: N/A

Description: Grants for payment of hospital bills
Restrictions: Limited to residents of Merrimack, Hillsborough County, New Hampshire
$ Given: Four Grants totalling $11,000 area awarded to individuals; range, $2,221 - $3,370.
Application Information: Write for guidelines.
Deadline: None.
Contact: S. Robert Winer, Trustee

• • • • • • • • • • • • • • • • • • • •

NEW JERSEY

The de Kay Foundation
c/o Manufacturers Hanover
Trust Company
270 Park Ave.
New York, NY 10017
(212) 270-6000

Description: Grants to elderly individuals in financial need; particularly to those who are sick or disabled or who lack proper care.
Restrictions: Limited to residents of New York, New Jersey and Connecticut.
$ Given: In FY89, 83 grants totaling $202,540 were awarded to individuals; range, $350 - $7,150; general range, $1,000 - $5,000.
Application Information: Initial approach by letter; formal application required.
Deadline: None.
Contact: Lloyd Saltus II, Vice President

Otto Sussman Trust
P.O. Box 1374
Trainsmeadow Station
Flushing, NY 11370-9998
phone: N/A

Description: Financial assistance for medical bills and caregiving expenses to individuals with serious or terminal illnesses
Restrictions: Limited to residents of New York, New Jersey, Oklahoma, and Pennsylvania
$ Given: Grants range from $329 - $4,000
Application Information: Write letter requesting applications form and guidelines; explain circumstances of need; formal application required.
Deadline: None.
Contact: Edward S. Miller, Trustee

NEW YORK

The James Gordon Bennett Memorial Corporation
c/o New York Daily News
220 East 42nd St.
New York, NY 10017
phone: N/A

Description: Grants to journalists who have been employees of a daily New York City newspaper for ten years or more. Acceptance based on need. Funds to be used for "the physical needs of persons . . . who, by reason of old age, accident or bodily infirmity, or through lack of means, are unable to care for themselves."
Restrictions: Priority given to journalists who have worked int he borough of Manhattan.
$ Given: Grants range from $150 - $6,000.
Application Information: Write for guidelines and program information; formal application required.
Deadline: None
Contact: Denise Houseman

37

PRIVATE FOUNDATION FUNDING

· · · · · · · · · · · · · · · · · · · ·

Brockway Foundation for the Needy of the Village and Township of Homer, New York
c/o Key Bank
25 South Main St.
Homer, NY 13077-1314
phone: N/A

Description: Financial assistance based on need.
Restrictions: Limited to residents of the Homer, New York area.
$ Given: Grants range from $180 - $600
Application Information: Write for guidelines
Deadline: None.
Contact: M. Lee Swartwout, Treasurer

Milton Carpenter Foundation, Inc.
c/o Schutte
P.O. Box 226
Jefferson Valley, NY 12602-0509
(914) 621-2819

Description: Scholarships to students who have alcohol impairment in their immediate families.
Restrictions: Limited to students of Westchester or Putnam counties, NY
$ Given: 9 grants to individuals totalling $39,000; range, $1,500 - $6,000
Application Information: Include SAT scores and writing sample.
Deadline: February 1
Contact: Philip Shatz, Secretary

The Clark Foundation
30 Wall St.
New York, NY 10005
(212) 269-1833

Description: Financial aid of medical and hospital care to needy individuals in upstate New York and New York City
Restrictions: Limited to residents of upstate New York City
$ Given: In FY89, 18 grants totalling $108,330 were awarded to individuals; range, $560 - $15,600
Application Information: Write for guidelines.
Deadline: None.
Contact: Edward W. Stack, Secretary

Josiah H. Danforth Memorial Fund
8 Fremont St.
Gloversville, NY 12078
phone: N/A

Description: Financial aid for medical care.
Restrictions: Limited to residents of Fulton County, New York
$ Given: In 1989, 95 grants totaling $18,610 were awarded to individuals; range, $16, - 4500; average, $200; maximum grant per year per person, $500
Application Information: Write for guidelines, application form; formal application required.
Deadline: None.
Contact: N/A

The de Kay Foundation
c/o Manufacturers Hanover
Trust Company
270 Park Ave.
New York, NY 10020
(212) 270-600

Description: Grants to elderly individuals in financial need, particularly to those who are sick or disabled or who lack proper care.
Restrictions: Limited to residents of New York, New Jersey and Connecticut
$ Given: In FY89, 83 grants totaling $202,540 were awarded to individuals; range, $350 - $7,150 general range, $1,000 - $5,000
Application Information: Initial approach by letter; formal application required
Deadline: None
Contact: Lloyd Saltus II, Vice President

Adolph and Esther Gottlieb Foundation, Inc.
380 West Broadway
New York, NY 10012
(212) 226-0581

Description: Emergency assistance to visual artists due to unforeseen and catastrophic circumstances, including medical expenses, and grants to support artists' work.
Restrictions: Emergency aid limited to artists who have at least 10 years at a mature level of their work; grants are on one-time basis.
$ Given: Maximum grant is $5,000; average grant is $3,000.
Application Information: Initial approach by telephone to obtain application for Emergency Assistance Program
Deadline: None
Contact: Sanford Hirsch, Secretary

Mary W. MacKinnon Fund
c/o Wilber National Bank
Trust Department
245 Main St.
Oneonta, NY 13820
phone: N/A

Description: Funding for medical, hospital, nursing home, and rehabilitative care for elderly and indigent residents of Sidney, New York
$ Given: Grants totaling $48,453 are awarded to individuals.
Application Information: Applications must be submitted through a physician or hospital.
Deadline: None
Contact: N/A

PRIVATE FOUNDATION FUNDING

. . . .

Saranac Lake Voluntary Health Association, Inc.
70 Main St.
Saranac Lake, NY 12983-1706
phone: N/A

Description: Provides funding of visiting nurse services for the elderly in Saranac Lake, New York as well as grants for dental services to students.
Restrictions: Limited to residents of Saranac Lake, New York
$ Given: In FY89, 3 grants totalling $42,120 were awarded to individuals; range, $4,498 - $31,613.
Application Information: Write for guidelines.
Deadline: N/A
Contact: N/A

St. Luke's Nurses Benefit Fund
47 Phillips Lane
Darien, CT 06820
phone: N/A

Description: Grants for needy graduates of St. Luke's School of Nursing
Restrictions: Limited to St. Luke's alumnae
$ Given: In FY89, one grant for $$2,000 was awarded.
Application Information: Formal application required.
Deadline: None
Contact: Martha Kirk, Trustee

Otto Sussman Trust
P.O. Box 1374
Trainsmeadow Station
Flushing, NY 11370-9998
phone: N/A

Description: Financial assistance for medical bills and caregiving expenses to individuals with serious or terminal illnesses
Restrictions: Limited to residents of New York, New Jersey, Oklahoma, and Pennsylvania
$ Given: Grants range from $329 - $4,000
Application Information: Write letter requesting application form and guidelines; explain circumstances of need; formal application required.
Deadline: None
Contact: Edward S. Miller, Trustee

VonderLinden Charitable Trust
c/o Leonard Rachmilowitz
26 Mill St.
Rhinebeck, NY 12572
(914) 876-3021

Description: Grants for financially distressed residents of upstate New York; funds may be used to meet a variety of needs, including medical bills.
Restrictions: Limited to residents of upstate New York
$ Given: In FY89, 101 grants totaling $23,260 were awarded to individuals; range, $4 - $540
Application Information: Write or call for guidelines
Deadline: None
Contact: Leonard Rachmilowitz

Emma Reed Webster Aid Association, Inc.
c/o Frances E. Peglow
Rd. No. 2
Albion, NY 14411
phone: N/A

Description: Funding for health and general welfare
Restrictions: Limited to residents of Orleans County, NY
$ Given: 61 grants to individuals totaling $39,274; range, $40 - $1,080
Application Information: N/A
Deadline: N/A
Contact: N/A

OHIO

Christian Business Cares Foundation
P.O. Box 360691
Cleveland, OH 44136
(216) 621-0096

Description: One time grants for life-threatening medical emergencies
Restrictions: Limited to residents of northeast Ohio. Awards determined on basis of the effect of grant on applicant's overall condition
$ Given: Grants range for $8 - $10,000; average, $270
Application Information: Write for guidelines, brochure and newsletter; formal application required; interviews required.
Deadline: None
Contact: N/A

PRIVATE FOUNDATION FUNDING

· · · · · · · · · · · · · · · · · ·

Columbus Female Benevolent Society
228 South Drexel Ave.
Columbus, OH 43209
phone: NA

Description: Direct aid to pensioned widows
Restrictions: Limited to widows are residents of Franklin County, Ohio
$ Given: In 1989, an unspecified number of grants totaling $32,800 were awarded to individuals.
Application Information: No direct applications; recipients are referred by people in the community who are familiar with their circumstances.
Deadline: N/A
Contact: N/A

The Ford (S.N. and Ada) Fund
c/o Society Bank & Trust
P.O Box 849
Mansfield, OH 44901
(419) 525-7676

Description: Grants for hospitalization and care of the aged and incurably ill.
Restrictions: Limited to residents of Richland County, Ohio
$ Given: Grants range from $23 - $11,470
Application Information: Write for guidelines and annual report
Deadline: N/A
Contact: Nick Gesouras, Regional Trust Officer

Meshech Frost Testamentary Trust
109 South Washington St.
Tiffin, OH 44883
phone: N/A

Description: Grants to Tiffin, Ohio residents who are in financial need
Restrictions: Limited to resident of Tiffin, Ohio
$ Given: Grants range from $169 - $690
Application Information: Submit letter stating reasons for request
Deadline: None
Contact: Kenneth H. Myers, Secretary-Treasurer

Paul Motry Memorial Fund
c/o Dean S. Lucal
P.O. Box 357
Sandusky, OH 44870-0357
phone: N/A

Description: Funding for health services, and hospitals.
Restrictions: Limited to residents of Erie and western Ottawa counties, OH
$ Given: 78 grants to individuals totaling $29,910; range, $17 - $2,824
Application Information: Initial approach by application for assistance and doctor's letter
Deadline: N/A
Contact: N/A

• • • • • • • • • • • • • • • • • •

James R. Nicholl Memorial Foundation
c/o The Central Trust
Company of Northern Ohio
Trust Department
1949 Broadway
Lorain, OH 44052
(216) 244-1906

Description: Financial assistance for medical and surgical services to needy children (2 to 21 years of age). Grants paid directly to health care providers.
Restrictions: Limited to children who have been residents of Lorain County, Ohio for at least two years.
$ Given: In 1989, 11 medical assistance grants totaling $26,550 were awarded to individuals; range, $14 - $4,040.
Application Information: Write for information brochure and application guidelines; indicate medical need; formal application required.
Deadline: None.
Contact: David E. Nocjar, Trust Officer

Richman Brothers Foundation
P.O. Box 657
Chagrin Falls, OH 44022
(216) 247-5426

Description: Funding primarily for health care and children's agencies for residents of Ohio, especially Cleveland
$ Given: 168 grants to individuals totaling $44,705; range, $125 - $1,580
Application Information: Initial approach by proposal.
Deadline: October 15
Contact: Richard R. Moore, President

Virginia Wright Mothers Guild, Inc.
426 Clinton St.
Columbus, OH 43202-2741
phone: N/A

Description: Grants to aged women in financial need
Restrictions: Strictly limited to female residents of Columbus, Ohio
$ Given: Grants totaling $9,924 are awarded to individuals
Application Information: Write for guidelines
Deadline: N/A
Contact: M. Courtwright

PRIVATE FOUNDATION FUNDING

. . . .

OKLAHOMA

Otto Sussman Trust
P.O. Box 1374
Trainsmeadow Station
Flushing, NY 11370-9998
phone: N/A

Description: Financial assistance for medical bills and caregiving expenses to individuals with serious or terminal illnesses
Restrictions: Limited to residents of New York, New Jersey, Oklahoma, and Pennsylvania
$ Given: Grants range from $329 - $4,000
Application Information: Write letter requesting application form and guidelines; explain circumstances of need; formal application required.
Deadline: None
Contact: Edward S. Miller, Trustee

OREGON

The Elizabeth Church Clarke Testamentary Trust/ Fund Foundation
U.S. National Bank of Oregon
P.O. Box 3168
Portland, OR 97208
(503) 228-9405
APPLICATION ADDRESS:
Scottish Rite Temple
709 S.W. 15th Ave.
Portland, OR 97205

Description: Grants for medical assistance. Payment may be made directly to the individuals or the physicians and hospitals providing services.
Restrictions: Limited to residents of Oregon.
$ Given: In 1989, total giving was $32,770
Application Information: Initial approach by letter detailing needs and costs
Deadline: None
Contact: G.L. Selmyhr, Executive Secretary

Clarke (Louis G. & Elizabeth L.) Endowment Fund
U.S. National Bank of Oregon
P.O. Box 3168
Portland, OR 97208
(503) 228-9405
APPLICATION ADDRESS:
Scottish Rite Temple
709 S.W. 15th Ave.
Portland, OR 97205

Description: Grants to needy Masons or their immediate family who require hospitalization in the Portland, Oregon metropolitan area (Multnomah, Clackamas and Washington Counties)
Restrictions: Limited to Masons and their immediate families
$ Given: In FY89, an unspecified number of grants totaling $34,380 were awarded to individuals.
Application Information: Write for guidelines.
Deadline: N/A
Contact: G.L. Selmyhr, Executive Secretary

• • • • • • • • • • • • • • • • • • •

Blanche Fisher Foundation
1001 S.W. Fifth Ave., Ste. 1550
Portland, OR 97204
(503) 323-9111

Description: Financial aid for physically handicapped persons in Oregon
Restrictions: Limited to Oregon residents who have demonstrated financial need and who are disabled or physically handicapped
$ Given: In 1989, 148 grants totalling $70,190 were awarded to individuals; range, $25 - $1,500; general range, $100 - $1,000; average, $410.
Application Information: Write for application guidelines; formal application required
Deadline: None
Contact: William K. Shepherd, President

Sophia Byers McComas Foundation
c/o U.S. National Bank of Oregon
P.O. Box 3168
Portland, OR 97208
(503) 275-6564

Description: Grants to elderly and indigent residents of Oregon who are not receiving welfare assistance.
Restrictions: Limited to residents of Oregon
$ Given: In FY89, an unspecified number grants totaling $72,222 were awarded to individuals.
Application Information: Individuals may not apply directly; applicants are recommended to the trustees by various church groups, service agencies, etc.
Deadline: N/A
Contact: U.S. National Bank of Oregon, Trustee

Scottish Rite Oregon Consistory Almoner Fund, Inc.
Scottish Rite Temple
709 S.W. 15th Ave.
Portland, OR 97205
(503) 228-9405

Description: Assistance to financially distressed Masons and their families to help meet medical expenses.
Restrictions: Limited to Masons and their wives, widows and children who are residents of the state of Oregon.
$ Given: In FY89, an unspecified number of grants totaling $19,440 were awarded to individuals.
Application Information: Write for guidelines.
Deadline: None.
Contact: Walter Peters

PRIVATE FOUNDATION FUNDING

• • • • • • • • • • • • • • • • • • • •

PENNSYLVANIA

Margaret Baker Memorial Fund Trust
Mellon Bank (East) N.A.
P.O. Box 7236
Philadelphia, PA 19101-7236
phone: N/A
APPLICATION ADDRESS:
P.O. Box 663
Phoenixville, PA 19460

Description: Financial aid to widows and single women over age 30 and handicapped children under age 14.
Restrictions: Limited to residents of the Phoenixville, Pennsylvania, area
$ Given: Grants range from $108 - $750
Application Information: Send a letter including the applicant's age, income, infirmity (if any), and other supportive material, plus the name of a person who can verify the request.
Deadline: Applications accepted throughout the year; awards are usually made in July and November
Contact: L. Darlington Lessig, Treasurer

Addison H. Gibson Foundation
Six PPG Pl., Ste. 860
Pittsburgh, PA 15222
(412) 261-1611

Description: Funds to cover hospital and. medical costs for individuals with "correctable physical difficulties"
Restrictions: Limited to residents of western Pennsylvania (with emphasis on Allegheny County)
$ Given: Grants range from $60 - $12,000
Application Information: Applicants must be referred by a medical professional. Formal application required. Medical professional must provide name, age, sex and address of person for whom funding is sought, describe the nature of recommended medical assistance, and provide the name of the patient's primary physician. Grants are made directly to the medical professionals/institution providing services. Write for further information; formal application required; interviews required.
Deadline: None
Contact: Charlotte G. Kisseeleff, Secretary.

Edward W. Helfrick Senior Citizens Trust
400 Market St.
Sunbury, PA 17801
phone: N/A

Description: Grants to senior citizens of the 107th Legislative District in Pennsylvania who are in need as a result of fire or illness
Restrictions: See above
$ Given: Four grants of $500 each were awarded to individuals
Application Information: Write for guidelines
Deadline: None
Contact: N/A

**Quin (Robert D. &
Margaret W.) Foundation**
Hazleton National Bank
101 West Brad St.
Hazleton, PA 18201
phone: N/A

Description: Grants for students in financial need; intended
to meet needs including medication costs.
Restrictions: Limited to individuals up to 19 years old who
are at least one-year residents of an area within a 10-mile
radius of Hazleton, Pennsylvania City Hall
$ Given: Grants range from $35 - $900
Deadline: Write for guidelines
Contact: N/A

Otto Sussman Trust
P.O. Box 1374
Trainsmeadow Station
Flushing, NY 11370-9998
phone: N/A

Description: Financial assistance for medical bills and
caregiving expenses to individuals with serious or terminal
illnesses
Restrictions: Limited to residents of New York, New Jersey,
Oklahoma, and Pennsylvania
$ Given: Grants range from $329 - $4,000
Application Information: Write letter requesting application
form and guidelines; explain circumstances of need; formal
application required.
Deadline: None
Contact: Edward S. Miller, Trustee

RHODE ISLAND

**Robert B. Cranston/
Theophilus T. Pitman Fund**
18 Market Sq.
Newport, RI 02840
(401) 847-4260

Description: Grants to the aged, temporarily indigent and
indigent people of Newport County, Rhode Island. Funds for
medical assistance, food, utilities, clothing and housing
Restrictions: Limited to residents of Newport County,
Rhode Island
$ Given: In FY89, an unspecified number of grants totaling
$6,850 were awarded to individuals.
Application Information: Interview or reference from a local
welfare agency required
Deadline: None
Contact: The Reverend D.C. Hambly, Jr., Administrator

47

• • • • • • • • • • • • • • • • • • • •

Inez Sprague Trust
c/o Rhode Island Hospital
Trust Bank
One Hospital Trust Plaza
Providence, RI 02903
(401) 278-8700

Description: Financial assistance and medical expenses for needy individuals
Restrictions: Limited to residents of Rhode Island
$ Given: In FY89, 23 grants totalling $6,000 were awarded to individuals; range, $79 - $1,500
Application Information: Initial approach by letter
Deadline: None
Contact: Trustee

SOUTH CAROLINA

Graham Memorial Fund
308 West Main St.
Bennettsville, SC 29512
(803) 479-6804

Description: Grants for medical assistance and general welfare
Restrictions: Limited to residents of Bennettsville, South Carolina
$ Given: In FY89, 37 grants totalling $11,200 were awarded to individuals; range, $200 - $500
Application Information: Formal application required
Deadline: June 1
Contact: Chairman

TENNESSEE

State Industries Foundation
P.O. Box 307
Old Ferry Rd.
Ashland City, TN 37015
(615) 244-7040

Description: Financial assistance to needy individuals in Tennessee, including State Industries employees
Restrictions: Limited to residents of Tennessee
$ Given: Grants range form $1 - $400; average, $150
Application Information: Write or call for guidelines
Deadline: None
Contact: Joseph P. Lanier, Manager

TEXAS

Dallas Cotton Exchange Trust
Dallas Cotton Exchange
c/o Mr. Joe Ferguson
Dixon Trust Company
3141 Hood Street, Ste. 600
Dallas, TX 75219
phone: N/A

Description: Financial aid to persons engaged or formerly engaged in the cotton merchandising business in Dallas, Texas, their employees and former employees, and the immediate families of the above when they are unable to work or, if able to work, unable to earn a sufficient amount to meet their needs.
Restrictions: See above
$ Given: Application Information: Formal application required
Deadline: None
Contact: Joe Ferguson

H.C. Davis Fund
P.O. Box 2239
San Antonio, TX 78298
phone: N/A

Description: Grants to assist infirm Masons living in the 39th Masonic District of Texas
Restrictions: See above
$ Given: Grants range from $200 - $3,075
Application Information: Write for guidelines
Deadline: None
Contact: N/A

The Kings Foundation
P.O. Box 27333
Austin, TX 78755
phone: N/A

Description: Grants to individuals in financial need
Restrictions: Intended primarily for residents of Texas
$ Given: Grants range from $50 - $250
Application Information: Initial approach by letter
Deadline: N/A
Contact: N/A

The Mary L. Peyton Foundation
Bassett Tower, Ste. 908
303 Texas Ave.
El Paso, TX 79901-1456

Description: Funding for health, welfare and education
Restrictions: Limited to legal residents of El Paso County, TX who are unable to obtain assistance elsewhere
$ Given: 1,226 grants to individuals totaling $187,789; range, $25 - $2,000
Application Information: Initial approach by letter; application form required
Deadline: None
Contact: James M. Day, Executive Administrator

PRIVATE FOUNDATION FUNDING

• • • • • • • • • • • • • • • • • • • •

VIRGINIA

**A.C. Needles Trust Fund
Hospital Care**
c/o Dominion Trust Company
P.O. Box 13327
Roanoke, VA 24040
phone: N/A

Description: Grants for hospital care to financially distressed individuals
Restrictions: Limited to individuals in the Roanoke, Virginia, area
$ Given: Grants range from $710 - $9,450
Application Information: Write for guidelines
Deadline: N/A
Contact: N/A

WASHINGTON

G.M.L. Foundation, Inc.
P.O. Box 848
Port Angeles, WA 93862
phone: N/A

Description: Grants to individuals who need medical help
Restrictions: Limited to residents of Clallam County, Washington
$ Given: Grants totaling $12,275 are awarded to individuals.
Application Information: Write for guidelines
Deadline: N/A
Contact: Graham Ralston, Secretary

George T. Welch Testamentary Trust
c/o Baker-Boyer National Bank
P.O. Box 1796
Walla Walla, WA 99362
(509) 525-2000

Description: Medical assistance for financially distressed individuals
Restrictions: Limited to residents of Walla Walla County, Washington
$ Given: In FY89, 29 welfare assistance grants totaling $21,980 were awarded to individuals; range, $53 - $1,500.
Application Information: Formal application required
Deadlines: February 20, May 20, August 20, November 20
Contact: Bettie Loiacono, Trust Officer

50

· · · · · · · · · · · · · · · · · · · ·

WEST VIRGINIA

Good Shepherd Foundation, Inc.
Rte. 4, Box 349
Kinston, NC 28501-9317
(919) 569-3241

Description: Financial assistance for medical expenses
Restrictions: Limited to residents of Trenton Township, West Virginia
$ Given: Grants range from $1,130 - $2,500
Application Information: Initial approach by letter; formal application required
Deadline: None
Contact: Sue White, Secretary-Treasurer

Jamey Harless Foundation, Inc.
Drawer D
Gilbert, WV 25621
(304) 664-3227

Description: Loans and grants to financially distressed families
Restrictions: Limited to residents of the Gilbert, West Virginia, area
$ Given: Distress grants totalling $4,720 are awarded to individuals; distress loans totalling $5,600 are made to individuals.
Application Information: Initial approach by letter; formal application required
Deadline: None
Contact: Sharon Murphy, Secretary

WISCONSIN

Edward Rutledge Charity
P.O. Box 758
Chippewa Falls, WI 54729
(715) 723-6618

Description: Grants and loans to needy residents of Chippewa County, Wisconsin
Restrictions: See above
$ Given: In FY90, 235 relief assistance grants totalling $16,285 were awarded to individuals; range, $5 - $600.
Application Information: Formal application required
Deadline: July 1
Contact: John Frampton, President

. . . .

WYOMING

The Gorgen (Peter and Anna) Fund Charitable Trust
141 South Main St.
Buffalo, WY 82834-1824
(307) 684-2211
ADDITIONAL ADDRESS:
c/o William J. Kirven
104 Fort St.
Buffalo, WY 82834
(307) 684-2248

Description: Financial assistance for medical, dental and optical services
Restrictions: Limited to children in Johnson county, Wyoming
$ Given: Grants range from $16 - $500; average, $100
Application Information: Write for guidelines
Deadline: None
Contact: Robert R. Holt, Trustee

Perkins (B.F. & Rose H.) Foundation
P.O. Box 1064
Sheridan, WY 82801
(307) 674-8871

Description: Funding for medical assistance to persons ages 2 to 20
Restrictions: Limited to individuals who have been residents of Sheridan County, Wyoming for the last two consecutive years, and who are between ages 2 and 20
$ Given: In 1989, 165 medical assistance grants totalling $50,097 were awarded to individuals; range, $21 - $1,800; general range, $25 - $1,000.
Application Information: Formal application required; obtain application forms from foundation; foundation will send separate form directly to attending physician for cost estimate; interviews required
Deadline: Application accepted throughout the year; completed application from must be submitted by individual and attending physician by the first week of the month prior to treatment
Contact: Margaret Sweem, Manager

● ●

PRIVATE FOUNDATION FUNDING, NO GEOGRAPHICAL RESTRICTIONS

Bendheim (Charles and Elsa) Foundation
1 Parker Plaza
Fort Lee, NJ 07024
phone: N/A

Description: Grants to individuals for charitable purposes, including aid to the sick and destitute
Restrictions: Applicants must be Jewish and in need of financial assistance
$ Given: In 1989, total giving was $171,880
Application Information: Write for guidelines
Deadline: N/A
Contact: N/A

Broadcasters Foundation, Inc.
320 West 57th St.
New York, NY 10019
(212) 586-2000

Description: Grants to needy members of the broadcast industry and their families.
Restrictions: See above
$ Given: Grants range from $1,800 to $2,400
Application Information: Formal application required
Deadline: None
Contact: N/A

Eagles Memorial Foundation, Inc.
4710 14th St. W.
Bradenton, FL 34207
phone: N/A

Description: Grants to children of deceased Eagles servicemen and women, law officers and firefighters for dental, medical and hospital expenses
Restrictions: Limited to children (under the age of 18 unmarried and not self-supporting) of members of the Fraternal Order of Eagles and the Ladies Auxiliary who have died from injuries or diseases incurred or aggravated while serving (1) in the armed forces, 92) as an enforcement officer, or (3) as a full-time or volunteer firefighter. Individual recipients receive funds for psychic, hospital or orthodontic bills, total not to exceed $5,000. No benefits paid for self-inflicted injuries, crime-related injuries, or illness/injuries related to drug or alcohol abuse.
$ Given: In FY88, an unspecified number of medical assistance grants totalling $13,420 were awarded to individuals
Application Information: Write for guidelines
Deadline: N/A
Contact: N/A

PRIVATE FOUNDATION FUNDING

**Lottie Sleeper Hill &
Josiah Sleeper Fund**
c/o Fidelity Bank
Broad & Walnut Sts.
Philadelphia, PA 19108
(215) 985-8712

Description: Funding for health services
$ Given: 56 grants to individuals totaling $30,112; range,
$16 - $3,380
Application Information: N/A
Deadline: None
Contact: N/A

The Hugel Foundation
824 Gravier St.
New Orleans, LA 70112
phone: N/A

Description: Grants for health and Catholic giving
$ Given: 1 grant to individual totaling $3,500
Application Information: N/A
Deadline: N/A
Contact: N/A

**Island Memorial Medical
Fund, Inc.**
c/o Richard Purinon
Main Rd.
Washington Island, WI 54246
phone: N/A

Description: Financial assistance to help cover medical
expenses for needy individual. Funds paid directly to
physicians or treatment facilities.
Restrictions: N/A
$ Given: Grants range from $630 - $8,760
Application Information: Write foundation for application
guidelines an current deadline information
Deadline: Varies
Contact: Richard Purinon

Jockey Club Foundation
40 East 52nd St.
New York, NY 10022
(212) 371-5970

Description: Grants to financially distressed individuals who
are legitimately connected with thoroughbred breeding and
racing.
Restrictions: See above
$ Given: In 1989, a total of $394,278 was awarded in
grants to individuals.
Deadline: None
Contact: Nancy Colletti, Secretary to the Trustees

Max Mainzer Memorial Foundation, Inc.
570 Seventh Ave., 3rd Fl.
New York, NY 10018
(212) 921-3865

Description: Grants to financially distressed members of the American Jewish KC Fraternity or their widows.
Restrictions: See above
$ Given: In FY89, 15 grants totalling $34,440 were awarded to individuals; range, $250 - $4,200
Application Information: Contact foundation for guidelines
Deadline: None
Contact: N/A

NFL Alumni Foundation Fund
c/o Sigmund M. Hyman
P.O. Box 248
Stevenson, MD 21153-0248
(301) 486-5454

Description: Financial assistance to disabled former National Football League alumni (prior to 1959), including grants for death benefits and medical expenses
Restrictions: See above
$ Given: 24 grants totalling $144,420 are awarded to individuals; eligible persons may receive grants that will supplement their total annual income by up to $12,000 with a $250/month minimum.
Application Information: Initial approach by letter
Deadline: None
Contact: N/A

Katharine C. Pierce Trust
c/o State Street Bank & Trust Company
P.O. Box 351
Boston, MA 02101
(617) 654-3357

Description: Financial assistance for needy women
Restrictions: See above
$ Given: In 1989, an unspecified number of grants totalling $33,500 were awarded to individuals; range, $250 - $5,000; average range, $1,000 - $5,000
Application Information: Initial approach by letter, include personal history, needs and financial condition
Deadline: None
Contact: Robert W. Seymour, Trust Officer

Corporate/ Employee Grants

• •

This chapter contains information about companies and corporations that provide grants or loans for their employees or former employees.

As in the chapter on Private Foundation Funding, the material is organized by state. In some cases, where a corporation has offices in several states, the corporation is listed only under the state in which its headquarters are located. Unless specified in the restrictions, this does *not* mean that monies are available only to employees within that state. Wherever possible, each listing includes a description of what the foundation funds, any restrictions, the total amount of money awarded annually, the number of grants or loans made annually, the range of monies given, the average size of an award, information on how to apply, deadline date(s), and name(s) of contact person(s).

If your company/corporation is not included in this chapter, check with an employee benefits representative or your personnel director to see if your company offers assistance in paying medical expenses.

CORPORATE/EMPLOYEE GRANTS

• • • • • • • • • • • • • • • • • • • •

ARRANGED BY STATE, ACCORDING TO CORPORATE LOCATION

CALIFORNIA

A.P.Giannini Foundation for Employees
c/o Bank of America
Personnel Relations, Dept.
No. 3650
P.O. Box 37000
San Francisco, CA 94137
(415) 622-3706

Description: Relief grants to help cover medical bills and other emergency expenses.
Restrictions: Limited to Bank of America employees and their families, and to employees of Bank of America subsidiaries.
$ Given: Three grants totaling $5,366 are awarded to individuals: range, $787 - $2,640.
Application Information: Submit letter of application, including reason for grant request, amount requested, and assessment of applicant's financial status.
Deadline: None
Contact: N/A

Clorinda Giannini Memorial Benefit Fund
c/o Bank of America
Trust Department
P.O. Box 37121
San Francisco, CA 94137
(415) 622-3650

Description: Emergency assistance grants for illness, accident disability, surgery, medical and nursing care, hospitalization, financial difficulties, and loss of income.
Restrictions: Limited to Bank of America employees.
$ Given: 25 grants totaling $27,926 are awarded to individuals, range, $35 - $6,226; general range, $800 - $2,000.
Application Information: Initial contact by letter.
Deadline: None
Contact: Susan Morales

• • • • • • • • • • • • • • • • • •

George S. Ladd Memorial Fund
c/o V.M. Edwards
633 Folsom St., Rm. 420
San Francisco, CA 94107
Phone: N/A

Description: Financial assistance grants, including funding for medical treatment.
Restrictions: Limited to elderly and retired employees of Pacific Bell, Nevada Bell and Pacific Northwest Bell
$ Given: Grants range from $1,271 - $4,450
Application Information: Write for guidelines
Deadline: N/A
Contact: N/A

MICHIGAN

Hudson-Webber Foundation
333 West Fort St., Ste. 1310
Detroit, MI 48226
(313) 963-7777

Description: Counseling services and last-resort financial assistance. Grants provided primarily in cases involving problems with physical or emotional health, and in financial emergencies.
Restrictions: Limited to employees and qualified retired employees of the J.L. Hudson Company.
$ Given: Grants range from $500 - $1,000.
Application Information: Formal application required for review by the foundation's trustees; interviews required.
Deadline: None.
Contact: Gilbert Hudson, President.

MISSOURI

Kansas City Life Employees Welfare Fund
3520 Broadway
Kansas City, MO 64111-2565
(816) 753-7000

Description: Medical assistance grants
Restrictions: Limited to Kansas City Life employees and their spouses and/or dependents
$ Given: Grants range from $950 - $3,313.
Application Information: Initial contact by letter.
Deadline: None
Contact: Dennis M. Gaffney

CORPORATE/EMPLOYEE GRANTS

• • • • • • • • • • • • • • • • • •

George S. Ladd Memorial Fund
c/o V.M. Edwards
633 Folsom St., Rm. 420
San Francisco, CA 94107
phone: NA

Description: Financial assistance grants, including funding for medical treatment
Restrictions: Limited to elderly and retired employees of Pacific Bell, Nevada Bell and Pacific Northwest Bell
$ Given: Grants range from $1,271 - $4,450
Application Information: Write for guidelines.
Deadline: N/A
Contact: N/A

NEW YORK

Hegeman Memorial Trust Fund
One Madison Ave., Area 23VW
New York, NY 10010
APPLICATION ADDRESS:
Employee Advisory Services
One Madison Ave., Area 1MVW
New York, NY 10010
(212) 578-5584

Description: Grants for health and welfare
Restrictions: Limited to employees, active and retired, and their New York dependents, including dependents of deceased employees, of Metropolitan Life Insurance Company and its affiliates.
$ Given: 27 grants totaling $88,202 are given to individuals; range, $600 - $8,300.
Application Information: Initial approach by letter including financial statement to demonstrate need.
Deadline: None
Contact: Lott M. Maroney

OREGON

George S. Ladd Memorial Fund
c/o V.M. Edwards
633 Folsom St., Rm. 420
San Francisco, CA 94107
phone: NA

Description: Financial assistance grants, including funding for medical treatment
Restrictions: Limited to elderly and retired employees of Pacific Bell, Nevada Bell and Pacific Northwest Bell
$ Given: Grants range from $1,271 - $4,450
Application Information: Write for guidelines.
Deadline: N/A
Contact: N/A

● ● ● ● ● ● ● ● ● ● ● ● ● ● ● ● ● ●

TEXAS

Amon G. Carter Star Telegram Employees Fund
P.O. Box 17480
Fort Worth, TX 76102
(817) 332-3535

Description: Medical/hardship and pension supplement.
Restrictions: Limited to employees of the Fort Worth Star-Telegram, KXAS-TV, and WBAP-Radio
$ Given: 28 Welfare assistance grants totaling $233,017 are awarded; range, $844 - $7,964.
Application Information: Initial contact by letter.
Deadline: None.
Contact: Nenetta Taum, President

WASHINGTON

George S. Ladd Memorial Fund
c/o V.M. Edwards
633 Folsom St., Rm. 420
San Francisco, CA 94107
phone: NA

Description: Financial assistance grants, including funding for medical treatment
Restrictions: Limited to elderly and retired employees of Pacific Bell, Nevada Bell and Pacific Northwest Bell
$ Given: Grants range from $1,271 - $4,450
Application Information: Write for guidelines.
Deadline: N/A
Contact: N/A

Flow-through Funding

. . . .

Many foundations will give monies to individuals indirectly; that is, individuals must apply under the auspices of a nonprofit organization. Grants are paid directly to a medical institution (i.e., hospital, medical center, clinic) or nonprofit organization (i.e., disease association) for the benefit of individuals in financial need.

How do you go about applying for this type of funding? Check with your hospital, clinic, or medical center (you should contact the patient service representative; if there is none, check with the institution's business office to see who would be the appropriate person to contact). Ask the following questions:

1. "Do any of the flow-through foundations that I have chosen currently fund a program here at xyz hospital? If so, do I qualify?" If the answer to the first question is "no," then ask, "May I apply to these foundations under your auspices, with you as my sponsor?" If so, an appropriate member of the institution should be able to help you prepare the necessary application.

2. If the institution does not want to act as your sponsor, ask, "Is there another foundation-funded program here at xyz hospital for which I do qualify?"

FLOW-THROUGH FUNDING

•   •

Remember, medical institutions' business offices now do much more than preparing bills and asking for payment. They also serve as financial counselors, making sure patients clearly understand the institutions' financial procedures, and often they will offer assistance in tracking down sources of financial aid.

ALABAMA

The BE&K Foundation
2000 International Park Drive
Birmingham, AL 35243-4220
(205) 969-3600
APPLICATION ADDRESS:
P.O. Box 2332, Birmingham,
AL 35201

Description: Funding for drug abuse programs, education, and child development
Restrictions: Giving focused in Birmingham, Alabama
$ Given: In FY90, 48 grants totaling $174,000 were awarded; range of $25 - $50,000 per award
Application Information: Write for application guidelines; see the important information in the chapter introduction about the need for institutional affiliation.
Deadline: December
Contact: T. Michael Goodrich, Trustee

Herman and Emmie Bolden Foundation
P.O. Box 360028
Birmingham, AL 35236
(205) 252-5356

Description: Funding for health, hospitals, and denominational giving
Restrictions: Giving focused in Alabama
$ Given: 27 grants totaling $257,000 were awarded; range of $100 - $155,000 per award
Application Information: Write for application guidelines; see the important information in the chapter introduction about the need for institutional affiliation.
Deadline: None
Contact: Rachel Ziegler, Secretary

Central Bank Foundation
701 S. 20th Street
Birmingham, AL 35233

Description: Funding for community health, art, social services, and youth
Restrictions: Giving limited to Alabama
$ Given: 270 grants totaling $316,400 were awarded; range of $25 - $25,000 per award
Application Information: Write for application guidelines; see the important information in the chapter introduction about the need for institutional affiliation.
Deadline: N/A
Contact: Terence C. Brannon, President

FLOW-THROUGH FUNDING

• •

The Daniel Foundation of Alabama
200 Office Park Drive
Suite 100
Birmingham, AL 35223
(205) 879-0902

Description: Funding for health, education, social services, and culture
Restrictions: Giving focused in the Southeastern states, especially Alabama
$ Given: 26 grants totaling $1.33 million were awarded; range of $500 - $270,300 per award
Application Information: Write for application guidelines; see the important information in the chapter introduction about the need for institutional affiliation.
Deadline: None
Contact: S. Garry Smith, Secretary-Treasurer

The Florence Foundation
P.O. Box 2727
Mobile, AL 36652
APPLICATION ADDRESS:
P.O. Box 1403
Mobile, AL 36633
(205) 432-0980

Description: Funding for health associations and education
Restrictions: Giving focused in Alabama
$ Given: 8 grants totaling $139,400 were awarded; range of $1,000 - $50,000 per award
Application Information: Write for application guidelines; see the important information in the chapter introduction about the need for institutional affiliation.
Deadline: None
Contact: Dwain G. Luce, Trustee

The Greater Birmingham Foundation
P.O. Box 131027
Birmingham, AL 35213
(205) 933-0753

Description: Funding for health, welfare, culture, and social services
Restrictions: Giving focused in Birmingham, Alabama
$ Given: N/A
Application Information: Write for application guidelines; see the important information in the chapter introduction about the need for institutional affiliation.
Deadline: None
Contact: Mrs. William C. McDonald, Jr., Executive Director

• • • • • • • • • • • • • • • • • • •

Hill Crest Foundation
310 N. 19th Street
Bessemer, AL 35020
(205) 425-5800

Description: Funding for mental health services, health, hospitals, pharmacology, and education
Restrictions: Giving focused in Alabama
$ Given: 25 grants totaling $609,200 were awarded; range of $5,000 - $100,000 per award
Application Information: Write for application guidelines; see the important information in the chapter introduction about the need for institutional affiliation.
Deadline: None
Contact: Jack G. Paden, Chairman

Minnesota Mining and Manu-facturing Foundation, Inc.

For full description see listing under Minnesota

The Mobile Community Foundation
100 St. Joseph Street
Suite 416
Mobile, AL 36602
(205) 438-5591

Description: Funding for health and human services, education, and culture
Restrictions: Giving focused in Mobile, Alabama
$ Given: 139 grants totaling $1.37 million were awarded; range of $100 - $350,000 per award
Application Information: Write for application guidelines; see the important information in the chapter introduction about the need for institutional affiliation.
Deadline: October 1
Contact: Thomas H. Davis, Jr., Executive Director

The Sonat Foundation
1900 5th Avenue, North
P.O. Box 2563
Birmingham, AL 35202
(205) 325-7460

Description: Funding for health associations and services, education, social services, minorities, and the arts
Restrictions: Giving focused in Alabama, Connecticut, and Texas
$ Given: 307 grants totaling $1.07 million were awarded; range of $1,000 - $200,000 per award
Application Information: Write for application guidelines; see the important information in the chapter introduction about the need for institutional affiliation.
Deadline: None
Contact: Darlene Sanders, Secretary

FLOW-THROUGH FUNDING

. . . .

USX Foundation, Inc.

For full description see listing under Minnesota

**Vulcan Materials Company
Foundation**
P.O. Box 530187
Birmingham, AL 35253-0497
(205) 877-3229

Description: Funding for health care, welfare agencies, drug abuse programs, hospitals, women's causes, and several other concerns
Restrictions: Giving focused in areas of corporate facilities
$ Given: In FY90, 500 grants totaling $1.8 million were awarded; average range of $100 - $20,000 per award
Application Information: Write for application guidelines; see the important information in the chapter introduction about the need for institutional affiliation.
Deadline: N/A
Contact: Mary S. Russom, Secretary-Treasurer

ARIZONA

Hexcel Foundation

For full description see listing in California

J.W. Kieckhefer Foundation
116 E. Gurley Street
P.O. Box 750
Prescott, AZ 86302
(602) 445-4010

Description: Funding for health agencies, medical research, hospices, social services, and education
Restrictions: N/A
$ Given: 42 grants totaling $675,000 were awarded; range of $1,000 - $125,000 per award
Application Information: Write for application guidelines; see the important information in the chapter introduction about the need for institutional affiliation.
Deadline: Proposals accepted May through November
Contact: Eugene P. Polk, Trustee

**Margaret T. Morris
Foundation**
P.O. Box 592
Prescott, AZ 86302
(602) 445-4010

Description: Funding for mental health, medical research, social services, the arts, education, and several other concerns
Restrictions: Giving focused in Arizona
$ Given: In 1990, 69 grants totaling $1.23 million were awarded; average range of $1,000 - $25,000 per award
Application Information: Write for application guidelines; see the important information in the chapter introduction about the need for institutional affiliation.
Deadline: Proposals accepted May through November
Contact: Eugene P. Polk, Trustee

• • • • • • • • • • • • • • • • • • •

Ray Foundation   **For full description see listing under Washington**

The Wallace Foundation
3370 North Hayden Road
Suite 123-287
Scottsdale, AZ 85251
(602) 962-4059

Description: Special project funding for social services,
mental health services, and other human services
Restrictions: Giving restricted to Arizona
$ Given: In FY90, 16 grants totaling $256,000 were awarded;
range of $500 - $19,600 per award
Application Information: Write for application guidelines;
see the important information in the chapter introduction
about the need for institutional affiliation.
Deadlines: March 15 and September 15
Contact: Nancy Shaw, Executive Director

ARKANSAS

The Ross Foundation
1039 Henderson Street
Arkadelphia, AR 71923
(501) 246-9881
APPLICATION ADDRESS:
P.O. Box 335
Arkadelphia, AR 71923

Description: Funding for mental retardation, youth agencies,
education, conservation, and community development
Restrictions: Giving restricted to Arkadelphia and Clark
County, Arkansas
$ Given: In 1990, 35 grants totaling $322,400 were awarded;
average range of $1,000 - $10,000 per award
Application Information: Write for application guidelines;
see the important information in the chapter introduction
about the need for institutional affiliation.
Deadline: December 1
Contact: Ross M. Whipple, President

Wal-Mart Foundation
702 S.W. Eighth Street
Bentonville, AR 72716-0671
(501) 273-6504

Description: Funding for health and welfare, including
programs for drug abuse and alcoholism; support for
education
Restrictions: Giving focused in areas of corporate operations
$ Given: In FY90, 3236 grants totaling $6.34 million were
awarded; average range of $1,000 - $2,000 per award
Application Information: Write for application guidelines;
see the important information in the chapter introduction
about the need for institutional affiliation.
Deadline: N/A
Contact: Carrie Grammer, Assistant Director

FLOW-THROUGH FUNDING

• • • • • • • • • • • • • • • • • • •

CALIFORNIA

The Aerospace Corporate Contributions Program
2350 E. El Segundo Boulevard
M.S. MI-448
El Segundo, CA 90245
(213) 336-6515
APPLICATION ADDRESS:
P.O. Box 92957
Los Angeles, CA 90278

Description: Funding for human services, health care, welfare, culture, and education
Restrictions: Giving focused in greater Los Angeles and communities where employees live and work
$ Given: Grants totaling $101,000 were awarded
Application Information: Write for application guidelines; see the important information in the chapter introduction about the need for institutional affiliation.
Deadline: N/A
Contact: Janet M. Antrim, Coordinator, Community Support

The Ahmanson Foundation
9215 Wilshire Boulevard
Beverly Hills, CA 90210

Description: Funding for health, medicine, education, and the arts
Restrictions: Giving in southern California, with focus on Los Angeles
$ Given: 406 grants totaling $20.15 million were awarded; range of $300 - $1.85 million per award
Application Information: Write for application guidelines; see the important information in the chapter introduction about the need for institutional affiliation.
Deadline: None
Contact: Lee E. Walcott, Vice President and Managing Director

The R.C. Baker Foundation
P.O. Box 6150
Orange, CA 92613-6150

Description: Although primary funding emphasis is on education, some support is available for mental health, hospitals, health and social service agencies, and youth
Restrictions: N/A
$ Given: In 1990, 213 grants totaling $1.05 million were awarded; average range of $100 - $77,500 per award
Application Information: Write for application guidelines; see the important information in the chapter introduction about the need for institutional affiliation.
Deadlines: May 1 and October 1
Contact: Frank L. Scott, Chairman

• •

**The Solomon R. and
Rebecca D. Baker
Foundation, Inc.**
1901 Avenue of the Stars
Suite 1231
Los Angeles, CA 90067
(310) 552-9822

Description: Funding for medical research in mental health fields, including autism; support for care and therapy of autistic individuals; welfare support
Restrictions: Giving focused in California
$ Given: In FY90, 16 grants totaling $111,000 were awarded; range of $100 - $70,000 per award
Application Information: Write for application guidelines; see the important information in the chapter introduction about the need for institutional affiliation.
Deadline: None
Contact: Solomon R. Baker, President

**George and Ruth Bradford
Foundation**
P.O. Box E
San Mateo, CA 94402-0017

Description: Although primary funding emphasis is on education, some support is available for mental health programs and other human services
Restrictions: Giving focused in California
$ Given: In FY89, 15 grants totaling $139,000 were awarded; range of $1,000 - $30,000 per award
Application Information: Write for application guidelines; see the important information in the chapter introduction about the need for institutional affiliation.
Deadline: None
Contact: Rebecca Haseleu

**California Community
Foundation**
606 S. Olive Street
Suite 2400
Los Angeles, CA 90014-1526
(213) 413-4042

Description: Funding for social services, including programs for the mentally handicapped; support for health, education, culture, and civic affairs
Restrictions: Giving in Los Angeles, Orange, Riverside, San Bernadino, and Ventura counties of California
$ Given: Grants totaling $8.7 million were awarded; average range of $5,000 - $25,000 per award
Application Information: Write for application guidelines; see the important information in the chapter introduction about the need for institutional affiliation.
Deadline: None
Contact: Jack Shakely, President

FLOW-THROUGH FUNDING

. . . .

**Community Foundation of
Santa Clara County**
960 West Hedding
Suite 220
San Jose, CA 95126-1215
(408) 241-2666

Description: Funding for health and social services, including mental health programs; support for education, the arts, community development, and the environment
Restrictions: Giving focused in Santa Clara County, California
$ Given: In FY90, grants totaling $2.08 million were awarded; average range of $2,500 - $15,000 per award
Application Information: Write for application guidelines; see the important information in the chapter introduction about the need for institutional affiliation.
Deadlines: 12 weeks prior to board meetings; board meets January 1, July 1, and October 1
Contact: Winnie Chu, Program Officer

**James S. Copley
Foundation**
7776 Ivanhoe Avenue
P.O. Box 1530
La Jolla, CA 92038-1530
(619) 454-0411

Description: Funding in several areas of interest, including drug abuse programs, hospitals, social services, and education
Restrictions: Giving focused in areas of company newspaper circulation: San Diego, Torrance, San Pedro, and Santa Monica, California; and Aurora, Elgin, Wheaton, Joliet, Springfield, Lincoln, Naperville, and Waukegan, Illinois
$ Given: In 1990, grants totaling $1.78 million were awarded; average range of $500 - $10,000 per award
Application Information: Write for application guidelines; see the important information in the chapter introduction about the need for institutional affiliation.
Deadline: None
Contact: Anita A. Baumgardner, Secretary

S.H. Cowell Foundation
260 California
Suite 501
San Francisco, CA 94111
(415) 397-0285

Description: Funding for programs aiding the handicapped; support for alcohol abuse programs; funding for family planning projects
Restrictions: Giving focused in northern California
$ Given: N/A
Application Information: Write for application guidelines; see the important information in the chapter introduction about the need for institutional affiliation.
Deadline: None
Contact: Stephanie Wolf, Executive Director

Dr. Seuss Foundation
7301 Encelia Drive
La Jolla, CA 92037
(619) 454-7384

Description: Funding for mental health, hospitals, health associations, medical research, and other human services
Restrictions: Giving focused in California
$ Given: In 1990, 92 grants totaling $165,000 were awarded; range of $25 - $22,400 per award
Application Information: Write for application guidelines; see the important information in the chapter introduction about the need for institutional affiliation.
Deadline: None
Contact: Robert L. Bernstein, Vice President

Joseph Drown Foundation
1999 Avenue of the Stars
No. 1930
Los Angeles, CA 90067
(310) 277-4488

Description: Funding for health services, drug abuse programs, and education
Restrictions: Giving focused in California
$ Given: In FY90, 159 grants totaling $3.57 million were awarded; average range of $5,000 - $25,000 per award
Application Information: Write for application guidelines; see the important information in the chapter introduction about the need for institutional affiliation.
Deadlines: January 15, April 15, July 15, and October 15
Contact: Wendy Wachtell Schine, Vice President and Program Director

FLOW-THROUGH FUNDING

• •

**The Carl Gellert
Foundation**
2222 19th Avenue
San Francisco, CA 94116
(415) 566-4420

Description: Funding for drug abuse programs, medical research, education, hospitals, and several other concerns
Restrictions: Giving focused in the San Francisco Bay area of California
$ Given: In FY90, 108 grants totaling $638,500 were awarded; average range of $1,000 - $10,000 per award
Application Information: Write for application guidelines; see the important information in the chapter introduction about the need for institutional affiliation.
Deadline: October 1
Contact: Peter J. Brusati, Secretary

**Celia Berta Gellert
Foundation**
2222 19th Avenue
San Francisco, CA 94116-
1896
(415) 566-4420

Description: Funding for social services, including drug abuse programs; support for hospitals, education, Catholic churches, medical research, and other concerns
Restrictions: Giving focused in the San Francisco Bay area of California
$ Given: In FY90, 32 grants totaling $168,500 were awarded; average range of $2,500 - $5,000 per award
Application Information: Write for application guidelines; see the important information in the chapter introduction about the need for institutional affiliation.
Deadline: October 1
Contact: Peter J. Brusati, Secretary

**Greater Santa Cruz
Community Foundation**
820 Bay Avenue
Suite 204
Capitola, CA 95010
(408) 662-8290

Description: Funding for health, social services, education, and culture
Restrictions: Giving focused in Santa Cruz County, California
$ Given: 148 grants totaling $178,800 were awarded
Application Information: Write for application guidelines; see the important information in the chapter introduction about the need for institutional affiliation.
Deadlines: March 31 and September 30
Contact: Grace Jepsen, Executive Director

• • • • • • • • • • • • • • • • • • • •

Harden Foundation
P.O. Box 779
Salinas, CA 93902-0779
(408) 442-3005
APPLICATION ADDRESS:
17 East Gabilan Street
Salinas, CA 93901

Description: Funding for mental health, hospitals, family planning, and other concerns
Restrictions: Giving restricted to Monterey County, California, with focus on the Salinas Valley area
$ Given: In FY90, 40 grants totaling $1.83 million were awarded; average range of $10,000 - $50,000 per award
Application Information: Write for application guidelines; see the important information in the chapter introduction about the need for institutional affiliation.
Deadlines: May 1 and November 1
Contact: Andrew Church, Secretary

Hexcel Foundation
P.O. Box 2312
Dublin, CA 94568
(415) 828-4200

Description: Funding for mental health and drug abuse treatment centers; support for health, welfare, youth, culture, and community projects
Restrictions: Giving in San Francisco, Dublin, Pleasanton, Livermore, City of Industry, Chatsworth, and San Diego, California; support also in areas of Arizona, Michigan, Nevada, Ohio, Pennsylvania, and Texas
$ Given: 42 grants totaling $104,800 were awarded; range of $125 - $25,800 per award
Application Information: Write for application guidelines; see the important information in the chapter introduction about the need for institutional affiliation.
Deadline: None
Contact: Karel Kramer Marriott, Manager of Corporate Contributions

Lucile Horton Howe and Mitchell B. Howe Foundation
180 South Lake Avenue
Pasadena, CA 91101-2619
(213) 684-2240
(818) 792-0535

Description: Research funding and continuing support for medical research, drug abuse rehabilitation programs, education, and social welfare
Restrictions: Giving focused in San Gabriel Valley and Prox-Pasadena, California
$ Given: In 1989, 49 grants totaling $151,400 were awarded; range of $100 - $75,000 per award
Application Information: Write for application guidelines; see the important information in the chapter introduction about the need for institutional affiliation.
Deadline: July 1
Contact: Mitchell B. Howe, Jr., President

FLOW-THROUGH FUNDING

• • • • • • • • • • • • • • • • • •

The Huffy Foundation, Inc.   **For full description see listing under Ohio**

Irvine Health Foundation
4199 Campus Drive
Suite 550
Irvine, CA 92715
(714) 854-6484

Description: Funding for community-based health care, including a drug abuse program and a senior care center
Restrictions: Giving restricted to Orange County, California
$ Given: In FY90, 9 grants totaling $948,500 were awarded; range of $10,000 - $540,600 per award
Application Information: Write for application guidelines; see the important information in the chapter introduction about the need for institutional affiliation.
Deadline: None
Contact: Edward B. Kacic, Executive Director

James Irvine Foundation
One Market Plaza
Spear Tower
Suite 1715
San Francisco, CA 94105

Description: Funding for drug/alcohol abuse programs, family planning, and other health and social services
Restrictions: Giving focused in California
$ Given: 273 grants were awarded; range of $5,000 - $2 million per award
Application Information: Write for application guidelines; see the important information in the chapter introduction about the need for institutional affiliation.
Deadline: None
Contact: Luiz A. Vega, Director of Grants Program

Irwin J. Jaeger Foundation
c/o Barbara S. Bromberg
1700 Central Trust Tower
Cincinnati, OH 45202
APPLICATION ADDRESS:
P.O. Box 67736, Los Angeles,
CA 90067

Description: Funding for mental health, psychology, youth/child welfare, Jewish giving, education, and the arts
Restrictions: Giving focused in southern California
$ Given: In FY90, 24 grants totaling $114,600 were awarded; range of $15 - $79,400 per award
Application Information: Write for application guidelines; see the important information in the chapter introduction about the need for institutional affiliation.
Deadline: N/A
Contact: Irwin J. Jaeger, President and Treasurer

The Jerome Foundation
4020 Bandini Boulevard
Los Angeles, CA 90023
APPLICATION ADDRESS:
2660 West Woodland Drive,
Suite 160, Anaheim, CA
92801
(714) 995-1696

Description: Funding for health agencies, medical research, hospitals, the blind, and handicapped children
Restrictions: N/A
$ Given: 17 grants totaling $147,400 were awarded; range of $100 - $124,500 per award
Application Information: Write for application guidelines; see the important information in the chapter introduction about the need for institutional affiliation.
Deadline: None
Contact: Pat Perry

The Samuel S. Johnson Foundation

For full description see listing under Oregon

The Henry J. Kaiser Family Foundation Quadrus
2400 Sand Hill Road
Menlo Park, CA 94025
(415) 854-9400

Description: Funding for health, medicine
Restrictions: Giving nationwide with emphasis on San Francisco, California
$ Given: Grants totaling $12.7 million were awarded
Application Information: Write for application guidelines; see the important information in the chapter introduction about the need for institutional affiliation.
Deadline: None
Contact: Karen P. Sparks, Proposal and Grants Manager

Andrew & Irene Madsen Charitable Trust
c/o Security Pacific Bank
P.O. Box 2511
Department 435H
Phoenix, AZ 85002

Description: General purpose funding for social services, alcoholism and drug abuse programs, education, and other human services
Restrictions: Giving focused in California
$ Given: In 1990, 8 grants totaling $232,600 were awarded; range of $15,000 - $75,000 per award
Application Information: Write for application guidelines; see the important information in the chapter introduction about the need for institutional affiliation.
Deadline: None
Contact: Wilbur S. Anderson, Trustee

FLOW-THROUGH FUNDING

• • • • • • • • • • • • • • • • • • • •

Margoes Foundation
57 Post Street
Suite 604
San Francisco, CA 94104
(415) 981-2966

Description: Funding for treatment of mentally ill individuals and for cardiac research
Restrictions: Giving focused in the San Francisco Bay area of California
$ Given: In FY91, 17 grants totaling $149,000 were awarded; average range of $5,000 - $10,000 per award
Application Information: Write for application guidelines; see the important information in the chapter introduction about the need for institutional affiliation.
Deadline: None
Contact: John S. Blum, Principal Manager

Della Martin Foundation
c/o Sheppard, Mullin, Richter
and Hampton
333 S. Hope Street
48th Floor
Los Angeles, CA 90071
(213) 620-1780

Description: Funding for organizations seeking cure and cause of mental illness
Restrictions: Giving focused in southern California
$ Given: Grants totaling $135,500 were awarded
Application Information: Write for application guidelines; see the important information in the chapter introduction about the need for institutional affiliation.
Deadline: None; proposals accepted late in the year
Contact: Laurence K. Gould, Jr.

**Minnesota Mining and Manu-
facturing Foundation, Inc.**

For full description see listing under Minnesota

**Montgomery Street
Foundation**
235 Montgomery Street
Suite 1107
San Francisco, CA 94104
(415) 398-0600

Description: General purpose funding in several fields of interest, including drug abuse and alcoholism treatment
Restrictions: Giving focused in California
$ Given: In 1990, 144 grants totaling $1 million were awarded; average range of $5,000 - $10,000 per award
Application Information: Write for application guidelines; see the important information in the chapter introduction about the need for institutional affiliation.
Deadline: Varies
Contact: Carol K. Elliott, Secretary-Treasurer

National Medical Enterprises Corporate Giving Program
11620 Wilshire Boulevard
P.O. Box 25980
Los Angeles, CA 90025
(213) 470-5486

Description: Funding for health and health quality improvement
Restrictions: N/A
$ Given: 1129 grants totaling $1.8 million were awarded; range of $100 - $200,000 per award
Application Information: Write for application guidelines; see the important information in the chapter introduction about the need for institutional affiliation.
Deadlines: March 1, June 1, September 1, and December 1
Contact: Dyanne H. Habegger, Director

Bernard Osher Foundation
220 San Bruno Avenue
San Francisco, CA 94103-5090
(415) 861-5587

Description: General purpose and special project funding for social services, with emphasis on drug abuse programs; support for the arts, education, and Jewish organizations
Restrictions: Giving restricted to Alameda, Contra Costa, Marin, San Mateo, and San Francisco counties, California
$ Given: In 1990, 127 grants totaling $4.17 million were awarded; average range of $2,500 - $25,000 per award
Application Information: Write for application guidelines; see the important information in the chapter introduction about the need for institutional affiliation.
Deadline: None
Contact: Patricia Tracy-Nagle, Executive Administrator

Pacific Telesis Foundation
Pacific Telesis Center
130 Kearny Street
Room 3351
San Francisco, CA 94108
(415) 394-3693

Description: Funding for education and human services, including drug abuse programs
Restrictions: Giving focused in California, Nevada, and other states in which Pacific Telesis Group has business interests
$ Given: In 1989, 350 grants totaling $8 million were awarded; average range of $2,000 - $50,000 per award
Application Information: Write for application guidelines; see the important information in the chapter introduction about the need for institutional affiliation.
Deadline: None
Contact: Thomas S. Donahoe, President

FLOW-THROUGH FUNDING

• • • • • • • • • • • • • • • • • • • •

Pasadena Foundation
16 North Marengo Avenue
Suite 302
Pasadena, CA 91101
(818) 796-2097

Description: Funding for alcohol and drug abuse programs, mental health and medical research, hospitals, health services, and several other concerns
Restrictions: Giving restricted to Pasadena, California
$ Given: In 1990, 191 grants totaling $628,600 were awarded; range of $50 - $40,000 per award
Application Information: Write for application guidelines; see the important information in the chapter introduction about the need for institutional affiliation.
Deadline: July 1
Contact: Josephine L. Stephen, Executive Director

The Patron Saints Foundation
P.O. Box 40706
Pasadena, CA 91114-7706
(818) 797-2303

Description: Funding for health care programs, including mental health, drug abuse, and alcoholism treatment
Restrictions: Giving restricted to the San Gabriel Valley, California
$ Given: In FY90, 22 grants totaling $175,200 were awarded; range of $1,500 - $15,000 per award
Application Information: Write for application guidelines; see the important information in the chapter introduction about the need for institutional affiliation.
Deadlines: Early March and early October
Contact: Jacquie Fennessy, Director

The PCS Foundation
c/o Ross Stores
8333 Central Avenue
Newark, CA 94560
(415) 845-9080

Description: Funding for Jewish welfare, social services, and health associations, including mental health associations
Restrictions: Giving in California, with focus on San Francisco and Stanford
$ Given: In FY90, 46 grants totaling $183,500 were awarded; range of $25 - $75,000 per award
Application Information: Write for application guidelines; see the important information in the chapter introduction about the need for institutional affiliation.
Deadline: None
Contact: Susan J. Moldaw

Peninsula Community Foundation
1204 Burlingame Avenue
P.O. Box 627
Burlingame, CA 94011-0627
(415) 342-2477

Description: Funding for health programs, emergency assistance, culture, and education
Restrictions: Giving restricted to Santa Clara and San Mateo County, California
$ Given: 15 grants totaling $2.3 million were awarded; range of $50 - $50,000 per award
Application Information: Write for application guidelines; see the important information in the chapter introduction about the need for institutional affiliation.
Deadline: None
Contact: Bill Somerville, Executive Director

Gustarus and Louise Pfeiffer Research Foundation
P.O. Box 1153
Redlands, CA 92373-0361
(214) 792-6269

Description: Funding for medicine and research, public health, and pharmacy
Restrictions: N/A
$ Given: 27 grants totaling $700,600 were awarded; range of $3,600 - $75,000 per award
Application Information: Write for application guidelines; see the important information in the chapter introduction about the need for institutional affiliation.
Deadline: N/A
Contact: George R. Pfeiffer, Secretary

Joseph H. and Florence A. Roblee Foundation

For full description see listing under Missouri

San Diego Community Foundation
525 B Street
Suite 410
San Diego, CA 92101
(619) 239-8815

Description: Funding for social services, education, culture, religion, and civic affairs
Restrictions: Giving focused in San Diego, California
$ Given: 373 grants totaling $2.04 million were awarded; range of $250 - $60,000 per award
Application Information: Write for application guidelines; see the important information in the chapter introduction about the need for institutional affiliation.
Deadlines: Bimonthly
Contact: Helen Monroe, Executive Director

FLOW-THROUGH FUNDING

• • • • • • • • • • • • • • • • • • • •

Annunziata Sanguinetti Foundation
c/o Wells Fargo Bank, N.A.
420 Montgomery Street
5th Floor
San Francisco, CA 94163
(415) 396-3215

Description: Funding for mental and physical health, drug abuse programs, child welfare, and other human services
Restrictions: Giving restricted to San Francisco, California
$ Given: In FY90, 48 grants totaling $226,700 were awarded; average range of $1,000 - $11,000 per award
Application Information: Write for application guidelines; see the important information in the chapter introduction about the need for institutional affiliation.
Deadline: October 31
Contact: Eugene J. Ranghiasci

Charles See Foundation
11100 N.E. Eighth Street
Suite 610
Bellevue, WA 98004
(206) 635-7250

Description: Funding for mental health, hospitals, education, religion, and other concerns
Restrictions: Giving focused in California
$ Given: In 1990, 32 grants totaling $100,200 were awarded; average range of $100 - $20,000 per award
Application Information: Write for application guidelines; see the important information in the chapter introduction about the need for institutional affiliation.
Deadline: November 14
Contact: Charles B. See, President

The Sierra Foundation
1211 Gold Country Boulevard
Suite 101
Rancho Cordova, CA 95670
(916) 635-4755

Description: Funding for health-related programs
Restrictions: Giving in California
$ Given: 64 grants were awarded; range of $600 - $168,400 per award
Application Information: Write for application guidelines; see the important information in the chapter introduction about the need for institutional affiliation.
Deadline: None
Contact: Len McCandliss, President

• •

Jennifer Jones Simon Foundation
411 West Colorado Blvd.
Pasadena, CA 91105
(818) 449-6840

Description: Annual campaign funding for mental health programs
Restrictions: Grants usually initiated by the foundation
$ Given: In FY90, 3 grants totaling $323,200 were awarded; average range of $300 - $300,000 per award
Application Information: Write for application guidelines; see the important information in the chapter introduction about the need for institutional affiliation.
Deadline: None
Contact: Walter W. Timoshuk, Vice President

Sonoma County Foundation
1260 N. Dutton Avenue
Suite 280
Santa Rosa, CA 95401
(707) 579-4073

Description: Funding for health and human services programs, arts, and culture
Restrictions: Giving focused in Sonoma County, California
$ Given: 60 grants totaling $341,000 were awarded; range of $250 - $5,000 per award
Application Information: Write for application guidelines; see the important information in the chapter introduction about the need for institutional affiliation.
Deadlines: June 1 and September 1
Contact: Virginia Hubbell, Executive Director

C.J. Stafford & Dot Stafford Memorial Trust
c/o San Diego Trust & Savings Bank
P.O. Box 129113
San Diego, CA 92112
(619) 557-3164

Description: Funding for social services, including alcohol and drug abuse programs, hospitals, health associations, and medical research
Restrictions: Giving restricted to San Diego County, California
$ Given: In FY90, 26 grants totaling $98,000 were awarded; average range of $500 - $20,000 per award
Application Information: Write for application guidelines; see the important information in the chapter introduction about the need for institutional affiliation.
Deadline: April 1
Contact: Jacquelyn Powers, Trust Officer, San Diego Trust & Savings Bank

FLOW-THROUGH FUNDING

• • • • • • • • • • • • • • • • • • • •

John and Beverly Stauffer Foundation, Inc.
P.O. Box 48345
Los Angeles, CA 90048
(213) 381-3933
APPLICATION ADDRESS:
P.O. Box 2246
Los Angeles, CA 90028

Description: Funding for alcohol and drug abuse programs, medical research, hospitals, education, and other human services
Restrictions: Giving focused in southern California
$ Given: In 1990, grants totaling $191,600 were awarded
Application Information: Write for application guidelines; see the important information in the chapter introduction about the need for institutional affiliation.
Deadline: None
Contact: Jack R. Sheridan, President

Irvin Stern Foundation

For full description see listing under Illinois

Glen & Dorothy Stillwell Charitable Trust
301 North Laile Avenue
10th Floor
Pasadena, CA 91101
(818) 793-9400

Description: Funding for social services, including drug and alcohol dependency programs
Restrictions: Giving restricted to Orange County, California
$ Given: In FY90, 9 grants totaling $88,600 were awarded; average range of $5,000 - $12,000 per award
Application Information: Write for application guidelines; see the important information in the chapter introduction about the need for institutional affiliation.
Deadline: None
Contact: Stanley C. Lagerlof, Chairman

Swift Memorial Health Care Foundation
P.O. Box 7048
Oxnard, CA 93031
(805) 385-3650

Description: Funding for drug and alcohol rehabilitation, health associations, and social services
Restrictions: Giving focused in Ventura County, California
$ Given: In FY91, 25 grants totaling $200,000 were awarded; average range of $100 - $20,000 per award
Application Information: Write for application guidelines; see the important information in the chapter introduction about the need for institutional affiliation.
Deadlines: April 30 and October 31
Contact: Emma M. Orr, Chair of Awards Committee

● ● ● ● ● ● ● ● ● ● ● ● ● ● ● ● ● ●

**Syntex Corporate
Contributions Program**
3401 Hillview Avenue
A6-164A
Palo Alto, CA 94304
(415) 855-6111

Description: Funding for health services, education, AIDS, medicine, science, arts, the handicapped, and community development
Restrictions: Giving focused in Santa Clara County, California
$ Given: Grants totaling $2.55 million were awarded; range of $1,000 - $15,000 per award
Application Information: Write for application guidelines; see the important information in the chapter introduction about the need for institutional affiliation.
Deadline: None
Contact: Frank Koch, Director, Corporate Contributions

Toyota USA Foundation
19001 S. Western Avenue
Torrance, CA 90509
(213) 618-6766

Description: Funding for health, community programs, minorities, youth, culture, and education
Restrictions: N/A
$ Given: 9 grants totaling $220,000 were awarded; range of $15,000 - $45,000 per award
Application Information: Write for application guidelines; see the important information in the chapter introduction about the need for institutional affiliation.
Deadlines: February 15, May 15, August 15, and November 15
Contact: Kimberly Byron

Transamerica Foundation
600 Montgomery Street
San Francisco, CA 94111
(415) 983-4333

Description: Funding for drug abuse programs, alcoholism programs, AIDS programs, and other concerns
Restrictions: Giving focused in the San Francisco Bay area of California
$ Given: In 1990, grants totaling $1.33 million were awarded; average range of $250 - $55,000 per award
Application Information: Write for application guidelines; see the important information in the chapter introduction about the need for institutional affiliation.
Deadline: None
Contact: Mary Sawai, Administrative Assistant

FLOW-THROUGH FUNDING

• • • • • • • • • • • • • • • • • • • •

Eleanor Slate van Loben Sels Charitable Foundation
235 Montgomery Street
No. 1635
San Francisco, CA 94104
(415) 983-1093
APPLICATION ADDRESS:
P.O. Box 7880, Room 1635
San Francisco, CA 94120-7880

Description: Funding for innovative projects in several areas; support for chemical dependency programs
Restrictions: Giving focused in northern California
$ Given: In 1990, 62 grants totaling $439,000 were awarded; average range of $500 - $20,000 per award
Application Information: Write for application guidelines; see the important information in the chapter introduction about the need for institutional affiliation.
Deadline: None
Contact: Claude H. Hogan, President

Wynn Foundation
P.O. Box 4370
Fullerton, CA 92634
(714) 449-8900

Description: Funding for alcohol and drug abuse programs, health, education, hospitals, medical research, and other concerns
Restrictions: Giving focused in Los Angeles County, San Gabriel Valley, and Orange County, California
$ Given: In 1989, 24 grants totaling $71,500 were awarded; range of $500 - $10,000 per award
Application Information: Write for application guidelines; see the important information in the chapter introduction about the need for institutional affiliation.
Deadline: Second Tuesday of March
Contact: Wesley E. Bellwood, President

COLORADO

Boettcher Foundation
600 17th Street
Suite 2210 South
Denver, CO 80202
(303) 534-1937

Description: Funding for health, including drug abuse rehabilitation; support for education, social services, urban development, and the arts
Restrictions: Giving restricted to Colorado
$ Given: In 1990, 120 grants totaling $3.23 million were awarded; average range of $10,000 - $50,000 per award
Application Information: Write for application guidelines; see the important information in the chapter introduction about the need for institutional affiliation.
Deadline: None
Contact: William A. Douglas, President

Ruth H. Brown Foundation
240 St. Paul Street
No. 100
Denver, CO 80206-5113
(303) 333-5309

Description: Operating and special project funding for health services, youth, and alcoholism treatment/research
Restrictions: Giving focused in Denver and Aspen, Colorado
$ Given: In 1989, 24 grants totaling $85,500 were awarded; range of $20 - $31,500 per award
Application Information: Write for application guidelines; see the important information in the chapter introduction about the need for institutional affiliation.
Deadline: None
Contact: Ruth H. Brown

Comprecare Foundation, Inc.
P.O. Box 441170
Aurora, CO 80044
(303) 322-1641

Description: Funding for health-related programs, including mental health programs
Restrictions: Giving focused in Colorado
$ Given: 16 grants were awarded; range of $2,000 - $46,000 per award
Application Information: Write for application guidelines; see the important information in the chapter introduction about the need for institutional affiliation.
Deadline: None
Contact: J.R. Gilsdorf, Executive Director

The Huffy Foundation, Inc.

For full description see listing under Ohio

The Curtis W. McGraw Foundation

For full description see listing under New Jersey

CONNECTICUT

Aetna Foundation, Inc.
151 Farmington Avenue
Hartford, CT 06156

Description: Funding for social services, education, minorities, and arts
Restrictions: Giving in areas of major Aetna field operations
$ Given: Grants totaling $8.14 were awarded; range of $300 - $1.16 million per award
Application Information: Write for application guidelines; see the important information in the chapter introduction about the need for institutional affiliation.
Deadline: None
Contact: Kelly Bedard

FLOW-THROUGH FUNDING

· ·

The Bingham Trust
21 Ann Street
Old Greenwich, CT 06870
(203) 637-2178

Description: Funding for programs that help psychiatric patients in transition from hospitalization to independent living (no funding for substance abuse patients); support for writing proficiency projects
Restrictions: N/A
$ Given: In 1990, 13 grants totaling $1.47 million were awarded; average range of $25,000 - $300,000 per award
Application Information: Write for application guidelines; see the important information in the chapter introduction about the need for institutional affiliation.
Deadline: N/A
Contact: Robert T. Barr, Trustee

Bodenwein Public Benevolent Foundation
c/o Connecticut National Bank
250 Captain's Walk
New London, CT 06320
(203) 447-6133

Description: Funding for health agencies and social services
Restrictions: Giving focused in Connecticut
$ Given: 36 grants totaling $220,000 were awarded; range of $700 - $32,000 per award
Application Information: Write for application guidelines; see the important information in the chapter introduction about the need for institutional affiliation.
Deadlines: May 15 and November 15
Contact: Mildred E. DeVine, Vice President, Connecticut National Bank

The Bridgeport Area Foundation, Inc.
280 State Street
Bridgeport, CT 06604
(203) 334-7511

Description: Funding for health and social services, including drug abuse programs; support for education and culture
Restrictions: Giving focused in Bridgeport, Easton, Fairfield, Milford, Monroe, Shelton, Stratford, Trumbull, and Westport, Connecticut
$ Given: In FY91, 300 grants totaling $792,000 were awarded; average range of $3,000 - $5,000 per award
Application Information: Write for application guidelines; see the important information in the chapter introduction about the need for institutional affiliation.
Deadlines: February 15, May 15, and September 15
Contact: Richard O. Dietrich, President and CEO

• • • • • • • • • • • • • • • • • • •

The Bulkley Foundation Trust
25 Forest Road
Weston, CT 06883-2307
(203) 227-8161

Description: Funding for health and social/welfare services, including alcoholism programs
Restrictions: Giving focused in Norwalk, Connecticut
$ Given: In 1990, 41 grants totaling $284,700 were awarded; average range of $500 - $25,000 per award
Application Information: Write for application guidelines; see the important information in the chapter introduction about the need for institutional affiliation.
Deadline: None
Contact: Kenneth M. Park, Trustee

The Frances L. & Edwin L. Cummings Memorial Fund

For full description see listing under New Jersey

Hartford Foundation for Public Giving
85 Gillett Street
Hartford, CT 06105
(203) 548-1888

Description: Funding for hospitals, social services, community services, youth, and education
Restrictions: Giving focused in greater Hartford, Connecticut
$ Given: 268 grants totaling $7.35 million were awarded; range of $250 - $250,000 per award
Application Information: Write for application guidelines; see the important information in the chapter introduction about the need for institutional affiliation.
Deadline: July 30 for health care grants
Contact: Michael R. Banser, Executive Director

Marion E. Kenworthy - Sarah H. Swift Foundation, Inc.

For full description see listing under New York

New Haven Foundation
One State Street
New Haven, CT 06510
(203) 777-2386

Description: Funding for social services, hospitals and health agencies, youth, and education
Restrictions: Giving focused in New Haven and the lower Naugatuck River Valley of Connecticut
$ Given: Grants totaling $4.8 million were awarded
Application Information: Write for application guidelines; see the important information in the chapter introduction about the need for institutional affiliation.
Deadlines: January, April, August, and October
Contact: Helmer N. Ekstrom, Director

FLOW-THROUGH FUNDING

. . . .

Olin Corporation Charitable Trust
120 Long Ridge Road
Stamford, CT 06904
(203) 356-3301

Description: Funding for drug abuse programs, health associations, hospitals, education, youth, and the environment
Restrictions: Giving focused in areas of corporate operations
$ Given: 537 grants totaling $1.56 million were awarded; range of $50 - $100,000 per award
Application Information: Write for application guidelines; see the important information in the chapter introduction about the need for institutional affiliation.
Deadline: Proposals accepted January through August
Contact: Carmella V. Piacentini, Administrator

Norma F. Pfriem Foundation, Inc.
961 Main Street
Bridgeport, CT 06604-4314
(203) 384-5850

Description: Funding for mental health, hospitals, health services, and culture
Restrictions: Giving focused in Connecticut
$ Given: In 1990, 7 grants totaling $155,400 were awarded; range of $1,000 - $32,000 per award
Application Information: Write for application guidelines; see the important information in the chapter introduction about the need for institutional affiliation.
Deadline: September 30
Contact: Vincent A. Griffin, Jr., Treasurer

The Sonat Foundation

For full description see listing under Alabama

Theodore & Vada Stanley Foundation
Eight Bluff Point
Westport, CT 06880
(203) 227-0859

Description: Funding for mental health; support for an alliance for the mentally disabled
Restrictions: N/A
$ Given: In 1989, 4 grants totaling $595,000 were awarded; range of $10,000 - $550,000 per award
Application Information: Write for application guidelines; see the important information in the chapter introduction about the need for institutional affiliation.
Deadline: None
Contact: Theodore Stanley, Trustee

• •

Swindells Charitable Foundation Trust
c/o Connecticut National Bank
777 Main Street
MSN242
Hartford, CT 06115
(203) 728-2274

Description: Funding for mental health and general health programs
Restrictions: Giving focused in Connecticut; funding emphasis on children's facilities
$ Given: In FY90, 10 grants totaling $64,000 were awarded; range of $2,000 - $20,000 per award
Application Information: Write for application guidelines; see the important information in the chapter introduction about the need for institutional affiliation.
Deadlines: February 18 and August 18
Contact: Amy Lynch, Trust Officer, Connecticut National Bank

The Waterbury Foundation
P.O. Box 252
Waterbury, CT 06720
(203) 753-1315

Description: Funding for health care, social services, education, and the arts
Restrictions: Giving focused in Waterbury, Connecticut
$ Given: 45 grants were awarded; range of $45 - $100,000 per award
Application Information: Write for application guidelines; see the important information in the chapter introduction about the need for institutional affiliation.
Deadlines: 7 weeks prior to board meetings in March, June, and November
Contact: Mrs. Ingrid Manning, Administrator

The Xerox Foundation
P.O. Box 1600
Stamford, CT 06904
(203) 968-3306

Description: Funding in several areas of interest; some support for drug abuse programs
Restrictions: Giving in areas of corporate operations
$ Given: In 1990, 1526 grants totaling $14.73 million were awarded; average range of $2,000 - $20,000 per award
Application Information: Write for application guidelines; see the important information in the chapter introduction about the need for institutional affiliation.
Deadline: None
Contact: Robert H. Gudger, Vice President

• • • • • • • • • • • • • • • • • • • •

DELAWARE

ICI Americas Corporate Giving Program
Public Affairs Department
Concord Pike and New Murphy Road
Wilmington, DE 19897
(302) 575-3000

Description: Funding for mental health, alcoholism and drug abuse programs, hospitals, health associations, AIDS, youth, and the arts
Restrictions: N/A
$ Given: Grants totaling $2.04 million were awarded
Application Information: Write for application guidelines; see the important information in the chapter introduction about the need for institutional affiliation.
Deadline: None
Contact: William C. Adams, Chairman

Little River Foundation

For full description see listing under Virginia

DISTRICT OF COLUMBIA

Charles S. Abell Foundation, Inc.

For full description see listing under Maryland

The Community Foundation of Greater Washington, Inc.
1002 Wisconsin Avenue, N.W.
Washington, DC 20007
(202) 338-8993

Description: Funding in many areas of interest, including health and substance abuse programs
Restrictions: Giving restricted to the Washington, DC metropolitan area
$ Given: In FY90, 357 grants totaling $5.03 million were awarded; average range of $1,000 - $10,000 per award
Application Information: Write for application guidelines; see the important information in the chapter introduction about the need for institutional affiliation.
Deadlines: May and October
Contact: Deborah S. McKown, Director of Finance

• • • • • • • • • • • • • • • • • • •

The Charles delMar Foundation
c/o Robert W. Alvord
918 16th Street, N.W.
No. 200
Washington, DC 20006
(202) 393-2494

Description: Funding in several areas of interest, including health and drug abuse programs
Restrictions: Giving in Washington, DC; Puerto Rico; and Latin America
$ Given: In 1990, 110 grants totaling $133,500 were awarded; range of $200 - $7,000 per award
Application Information: Write for application guidelines; see the important information in the chapter introduction about the need for institutional affiliation.
Deadline: None
Contact: Elizabeth Adams delMar, President

The Freed Foundation, Inc.
1202 Eton Court, N.W.
Washington, DC 20007
(202) 337-5487

Description: Funding for drug and alcohol abuse programs, mental illness programs, ecology, and animal welfare
Restrictions: Giving focused in Washington, DC and in New Jersey
$ Given: 39 grants totaling $608,700 were awarded; range of $1,000 - $200,000 per award
Application Information: Write for application guidelines; see the important information in the chapter introduction about the need for institutional affiliation.
Deadline: None
Contact: Lorraine Barnhart, Executive Director

GEICO Philanthropic Foundation
c/o Geico Corporation
Geico Plaza
Washington, DC 20076
(301) 986-2055

Description: Funding for health agencies, hospitals, education, culture, and community funds
Restrictions: N/A
$ Given: 275 grants totaling $765,500 were awarded; range of $25 - $138,000 per award
Application Information: Write for application guidelines; see the important information in the chapter introduction about the need for institutional affiliation.
Deadline: None
Contact: Carroll R. Franklin

FLOW-THROUGH FUNDING

. . . .

Giant Food Foundation, Inc.
P.O. Box 1804
Washington, DC 20013

Description: General purpose funding for health, including mental health, as well as for education, culture, Jewish welfare, and other concerns
Restrictions: Giving focused in Baltimore, Maryland and Washington, DC
$ Given: In FY90, 330 grants totaling $672,500 were awarded; range of $25 - $160,000 per award
Application Information: Write for application guidelines; see the important information in the chapter introduction about the need for institutional affiliation.
Deadline: None
Contact: David Rutstein, Secretary

The Joseph P. Kennedy, Jr. Foundation
1350 New York Avenue, N.W.
Suite 500
Washington, DC 20005
(202) 393-1250

Description: Funding for the prevention and care of mental retardation
Restrictions: N/A
$ Given: 27 grants totaling $1.6 million were awarded; range of $500 - $495,000 per award
Application Information: Write for application guidelines; see the important information in the chapter introduction about the need for institutional affiliation.
Deadline: October 1
Contact: Eunice Kennedy Shriver, Executive Vice President

Marion E. Kenworthy - Sarah H. Swift Foundation, Inc.

For full description see listing under New York

Marriott Corporate Giving Program
Marriott Drive
Washington, DC 20058
(301) 380-7430

Description: Funding in four areas - health and human services; education; civic programs; and the arts
Restrictions: Giving focused in Washington, DC and areas of Marriott corporate facilities
$ Given: N/A
Application Information: Write for application guidelines; see the important information in the chapter introduction about the need for institutional affiliation.
Deadline: None; proposals preferred in October
Contact: Judi A. Hadfield, Director, Corporate Relations Services

•   •

Eugene and Agnes E. Meyer Foundation
1400 Sixteenth Street, N.W.
Suite 360
Washington, DC 20036
(202) 482-8294

Description: Funding for mental health, welfare, education, health, and community services
Restrictions: Giving focused in metropolitan Washington, DC, including Virginia and Maryland
$ Given: 112 grants totaling $2.1 million were awarded; range of $250 - $100,000 per award
Application Information: Write for application guidelines; see the important information in the chapter introduction about the need for institutional affiliation.
Deadlines: April 1, August 1, and December 1
Contact: Julie L. Rogers, President

Walter G. Ross Foundation
c/o ASB Capital Management Inc.
655 15th Street, N.W.
Suite 800
Washington, DC 20005

Description: Funding for medical research, programs benefiting the mentally and/or physically handicapped, and other human services
Restrictions: Giving focused in Florida and Washington, DC
$ Given: In 1990, 19 grants totaling $372,500 were awarded; range of $2,500 - $100,000 per award
Application Information: Write for application guidelines; see the important information in the chapter introduction about the need for institutional affiliation.
Deadline: September 15
Contact: Ian W. Jones, Secretary

van Ameringen Foundation, Inc.

For full description see listing under New York

FLORIDA

Banyan Foundation, Inc.
c/o Duval-Bibb Co.
6605 Walton Way
Tampa, FL 33610-5516

Description: Funding to support research, treatment and education in mental health fields such as substance abuse, emotional health, trauma-related adjustment, family dysfunction, and stress
Restrictions: N/A
$ Given: In FY89, 48 grants totaling $112,200 were awarded; range of $25 - $50,000 per award
Application Information: Write for application guidelines; see the important information in the chapter introduction about the need for institutional affiliation.
Deadline: None
Contact: Reese Coppage, President

FLOW-THROUGH FUNDING

• •

Emil Buehler Foundation, Inc.

For full description see listing under New Jersey

Conn Memorial Foundation, Inc.
220 East Madison Street
Suite 822
P.O. Box 229
Tampa, FL 33601
(813) 223-3838

Description: Funding for alcoholism and drug abuse programs, as well as for education and youth agencies
Restrictions: Giving focused in Tampa Bay, Florida
$ Given: In FY90, 66 grants totaling $885,300 were awarded; average range of $1,000 - $20,000 per award
Application Information: Write for application guidelines; see the important information in the chapter introduction about the need for institutional affiliation.
Deadlines: May 31 and November 30
Contact: David B. Frye, President

Alfred I. DuPont Foundation
1550 Prudential Drive
Suite 400
P.O. Box 1380
Jacksonville, FL 32207
(904) 396-6600

Description: Funding for elderly adults in poor health, and for medical research
Restrictions: Giving focused in the southeastern United States
$ Given: 87 grants totaling $204,700 were awarded; range of $150 - $20,500 per award
Application Information: Write for application guidelines; see the important information in the chapter introduction about the need for institutional affiliation.
Deadline: None
Contact: Rosemary Cusimano, Assistant Secretary

The David Falk Foundation, Inc.
c/o SunBank of Tampa Bay
P.O. Box 1498
Tampa, FL 33601
(813) 224-1877

Description: Funding for drug abuse programs, social services, education, hospitals, youth, and other concerns
Restrictions: Giving focused in Tampa Bay, Florida
$ Given: In 1990, 27 grants totaling $105,200 were awarded; average range of $100 - $12,500 per award
Application Information: Write for application guidelines; see the important information in the chapter introduction about the need for institutional affiliation.
Deadline: Proposals accepted in January, April, July, and October
Contact: John J. Howley, Secretary-Treasurer

• •

**Charles A. Frueauff
Foundation, Inc.**
307 East Seventh Avenue
Tallahassee, FL 32303
(904) 561-3508

Description: Funding for health, mental health, hospitals, and related concerns
Restrictions: Giving on a national level
$ Given: In 1989, 169 grants totaling $3.2 million were awarded; average range of $10,000 - $25,000 per award
Application Information: Write for application guidelines; see the important information in the chapter introduction about the need for institutional affiliation.
Deadline: March 31
Contact: David A. Frueauff, Secretary

**Joseph and Sally
Handleman Charitable
Foundation**
c/o NBD Trust Co. of Florida
11300 U.S. Highway One
Suite 101
North Palm Beach, FL 33408
(407) 627-9400

Description: Funding for mental health, family services, education, and other concerns
Restrictions: Giving focused in Miami, Florida and New York
$ Given: In 1989, 25 grants totaling $160,000 were awarded; range of $2,500 - $20,000 per award
Application Information: Write for application guidelines; see the important information in the chapter introduction about the need for institutional affiliation.
Deadline: None
Contact: Gary W. Gomoll

**The ITT Rayonier
Foundation**
1177 Summer Street
Stamford, CT 06904
(203) 348-7000

Description: Funding for health, hospitals, education, and other civic responsibilities
Restrictions: Giving focused in Nassau County, Florida; Wayne County, Georgia; and various Washington counties
$ Given: 213 grants totaling $305,000 were awarded; range of $25 - $20,000 per award
Application Information: Write for application guidelines; see the important information in the chapter introduction about the need for institutional affiliation.
Deadline: November 30
Contact: Jerome D. Gregoire, Vice President

FLOW-THROUGH FUNDING

• • • • • • • • • • • • • • • • • • • •

Knight Foundation
One Biscayne Tower
Suite 3800
Two South Biscayne
Boulevard
Miami, FL 33131
(305) 539-0009

Description: Cities Program funding in several areas of interest, including mental health; additional support through Education Program, Journalism Program, and Arts and Culture Program
Restrictions: Cities Program giving focused in 26 communities where John S. and James L. Knight published newspapers
$ Given: In 1990, 395 grants totaling $23.15 million were awarded; average range of $5,000 - $100,000 per award
Application Information: Write for application guidelines; see the important information in the chapter introduction about the need for institutional affiliation.
Deadlines: January 1, April 1, July 1, and October 1
Contact: Lee Hills, Chairman

The Lost Tree Charitable Foundation, Inc.
11555 Lost Tree Way
North Palm Beach, FL 33408
(407) 622-3780

Description: Funding for social services, family services, alcohol and drug abuse programs, and other health services
Restrictions: N/A
$ Given: 30 grants totaling $146,400 were awarded; range of $500 - $14,500 per award
Application Information: Write for application guidelines; see the important information in the chapter introduction about the need for institutional affiliation.
Deadline: N/A
Contact: N/A

The Joe and Emily Lowe Foundation, Inc.
249 Royal Palm Way
Palm Beach, FL 33480
(407) 655-7001

Description: Funding for health services, hospitals, women's projects, medical research, education, the arts, and Jewish organizations
Restrictions: Giving focused in Florida, New York, and New Jersey
$ Given: 420 grants totaling $1.6 million were awarded; range of $250 - $100,000 per award
Application Information: Write for application guidelines; see the important information in the chapter introduction about the need for institutional affiliation.
Deadline: None
Contact: Helen G. Hauben, President

The Sumter and Ivilyn Lowry Charitable Foundation, Inc.
c/o First Florida Bank, N.A.
Trust Department
P.O. Box 31265
Tampa, FL 33631-3265
(813) 224-1570

Description: Funding for social services, drug abuse programs, child welfare, and other human services
Restrictions: Giving focused in Tampa, Florida
$ Given: In 1990, 28 grants totaling $108,000 were awarded; range of $1,000 - $25,000 per award
Application Information: Write for application guidelines; see the important information in the chapter introduction about the need for institutional affiliation.
Deadline: None
Contact: Florence Murphy

Joseph H. and Florence A. Roblee Foundation

For full description see listing under Missouri

The Retirement Research Foundation

For full description see listing under Illinois

Walter G. Ross Foundation

For full description see listing under District of Columbia

Schultz Foundation, Inc.
c/o Schultz Building
P.O. Box 1200
Jacksonville, FL 32201
(904) 354-3603
APPLICATION ADDRESS:
50 North Laura Street, Suite 2725, Jacksonville, FL 32202

Description: General purpose funding for drug abuse programs, culture, social services, education, and the environment
Restrictions: Giving focused in Jacksonville, Florida and Georgia
$ Given: In 1990, 110 grants totaling $122,000 were awarded; range of $20 - $10,000 per award
Application Information: Write for application guidelines; see the important information in the chapter introduction about the need for institutional affiliation.
Deadline: None
Contact: Clifford G. Schultz II, President

FLOW-THROUGH FUNDING

· ·

GEORGIA

Thomas C. Burke Foundation
182 Riley Avenue
Suite B
Macon, GA 31204
(912) 745-1442

Description: Funding for individuals suffering from disease, especially cancer
Restrictions: Giving focused in Georgia
$ Given: Grants totaling $177,200 were awarded
Application Information: Write for application guidelines; see the important information in the chapter introduction about the need for institutional affiliation.
Deadline: N/A
Contact: Carolyn P. Griggers

James M. Cox, Jr. Foundation, Inc.

For full description see listing under Ohio

Heileman Old Style Foundation, Inc.

For full description see listing under Wisconsin

The ITT Rayonier Foundation

For full description see listing under Florida

Mill Creek Foundation, Inc.
P.O. Box 190
Swainsboro, GA 30401
(912) 237-9971

Description: Special project funding for drug abuse programs, education, community development, and culture
Restrictions: Giving focused in Emanuel County, Georgia
$ Given: In 1990, 19 grants totaling $62,200 were awarded; range of $400 - $10,000 per award
Application Information: Write for application guidelines; see the important information in the chapter introduction about the need for institutional affiliation.
Deadline: N/A
Contact: James H. Morgan, Director

Minnesota Mining and Manufacturing Foundation, Inc.

For full description see listing under Minnesota

The Nordson Corporation Foundation

For full description see listing under Ohio

• • • • • • • • • • • • • • • • • • •

The Rich Foundation, Inc.
10 Piedmont Center
Suite 802
Atlanta, GA 30305
(404) 262-2266

Description: Funding for social services, including drug abuse programs; support for a community fund, the arts, education, and hospitals
Restrictions: Giving restricted to Atlanta, Georgia
$ Given: In FY90, 40 grants totaling $738,300 were awarded; range of $2,500 - $175,000 per award
Application Information: Write for application guidelines; see the important information in the chapter introduction about the need for institutional affiliation.
Deadlines: 6 weeks prior to board meetings; board meets in February, May, August, and November
Contact: Anne Poland Berg, Grant Consultant

Schultz Foundation, Inc.

For full description see listing under Florida

Trust Company of Georgia Foundation
c/o Trust Co. Bank, Atlanta
P.O. Box 4418
MC 041
Atlanta, GA 30302
(404) 588-8246

Description: Special project funding for health services, mental health services, community development, youth, and culture
Restrictions: Giving focused in metropolitan Atlanta, Georgia
$ Given: In 1990, grants totaling $1.15 million were awarded; average range of $3,000 - $5,000 per award
Application Information: Write for application guidelines; see the important information in the chapter introduction about the need for institutional affiliation.
Deadlines: March 1, June 1, September 1, and December 1
Contact: Victor A. Gregory, Secretary

HAWAII

The Barbara Cox Anthony Foundation
733 Fort Street, Suite 2000
Honolulu, HI 96813
APPLICATION ADDRESS:
P.O. Box 4316
Honolulu, HI 96813
(808) 536-1877

Description: Funding for mental health, social services, and education
Restrictions: Giving focused in Hawaii
$ Given: In 1989, 68 grants totaling $306,600 were awarded; average range of $100 - $5,000 per award
Application Information: Write for application guidelines; see the important information in the chapter introduction about the need for institutional affiliation.
Deadline: None
Contact: Garner Anthony, Vice President

FLOW-THROUGH FUNDING

• •

The Hawaii Community Foundation
222 Merchant Street
Honolulu, HI 96813

Description: Funding in 7 categories including youth, education, social services, learning disabled children, the elderly, mental health care, and the mentally ill
Restrictions: Giving limited to Hawaiian residents or individuals of Hawaiian ancestry
$ Given: 112 grants totaling $1.36 million were awarded; range of $5,000 - $200,000 per award
Application Information: Write for application guidelines; see the important information in the chapter introduction about the need for institutional affiliation.
Deadline: None
Contact: Suzanne Toguchi, Program Officer

Sophie Russell Testamentary Trust
c/o Bishop Trust Co., Ltd.
1000 Bishop Street
Honolulu, HI 96813
(808) 523-2233
MAILING ADDRESS:
P.O. Box 2390
Honolulu, HI 96804-2390

Description: General purpose funding for institutions caring for the mentally and/or physically handicapped; support for the Hawaiian Humane Society
Restrictions: Giving restricted to Hawaii
$ Given: In FY91, 14 grants totaling $85,000 were awarded; average range of $2,500 - $10,000 per award
Application Information: Write for application guidelines; see the important information in the chapter introduction about the need for institutional affiliation.
Deadline: January 15
Contact: Lois C. Loomis, Vice President, Bishop Trust Co., Ltd.

IDAHO

Boise Cascade Corporate Giving Program
One Jefferson Square
Boise, ID 83728
(208) 384-7673

Description: Funding for health and human services, hospitals, health and wellness promotion, education, the environment, and culture
Restrictions: Giving in areas of corporate operations
$ Given: Grants totaling $2.8 million were awarded
Application Information: Write for application guidelines; see the important information in the chapter introduction about the need for institutional affiliation.
Deadline: N/A
Contact: Vicki M. Wheeler, Contributions Manager

The Curtis W. McGraw Foundation

For full description see listing under New Jersey

• • • • • • • • • • • • • • • • • • • •

ILLINOIS

G.J. Aigner Foundation, Inc.
5617 Dempster Street
Morton Grove, IL 60053
(312) 966-5782

Description: Special project funding for innovative programs to enable the disabled and the mentally retarded to become self-supporting; support for mental/emotional therapy; funding for scholarships and welfare
Restrictions: N/A
$ Given: In FY90, 23 grants totaling $58,500 were awarded; range of $100 - $10,000 per award
Application Information: Write for application guidelines; see the important information in the chapter introduction about the need for institutional affiliation.
Deadline: None for special project funding or therapy
Contact: Craig P. Colmar, Director

The Barker Welfare Foundation

For full description see listing under New York

Francis Beidler Charitable Trust
53 West Jackson Boulevard
Room 530
Chicago, IL 60604-3608
(312) 922-3792

Description: Funding for social services, mental and behavioral sciences, education, foreign policy, and the environment
Restrictions: Giving focused in Illinois
$ Given: In 1990, 100 grants totaling $307,400 were awarded; range of $100 - $32,800 per award
Application Information: Write for application guidelines; see the important information in the chapter introduction about the need for institutional affiliation.
Deadline: None
Contact: Rosemarie Smith, Trustee

The Chicago Community Trust
222 North LaSalle Street
Suite 1400
Chicago, IL 60601
(312) 372-3356

Description: Funding for programs in health and social services, including mental health; research grants in mental retardation and developmental disabilities
Restrictions: Giving in Cook County, Illinois
$ Given: 600 grants totaling $25 million were awarded; range of $100 - $1 million per award
Application Information: Write for application guidelines; see the important information in the chapter introduction about the need for institutional affiliation.
Deadline: June 30 for research; none for other categories
Contact: Joan Miller Wood

FLOW-THROUGH FUNDING

• • • • • • • • • • • • • • • • • •

**James S. Copley
Foundation**

For full description see listing under California

DeSoto Foundation
P.O. Box 5030
1700 South Mt. Prospect
Road
Des Plaines, IL 60017

Description: Funding for health agencies, mental health programs, hospitals, and other human services
Restrictions: Giving focused in Illinois
$ Given: In 1989, 100 grants totaling $251,400 were awarded; range of $100 - $40,300 per award
Application Information: Write for application guidelines; see the important information in the chapter introduction about the need for institutional affiliation.
Deadlines: Before board meetings in March, August, and November
Contact: J. Barreiro, Vice President

Dr. Scholl Foundation
11 South LaSalle Street
Suite 2100
Chicago, IL 60603
(312) 782-5210

Description: Funding for programs for the developmentally disabled; support for hospitals, medical research, education, medicine and nursing
Restrictions: N/A
$ Given: 372 grants totaling $7.4 million were awarded; range of $1,000 - $200,000 per award
Application Information: Write for application guidelines; see the important information in the chapter introduction about the need for institutional affiliation.
Deadline: May 15
Contact: Jack E. Scholl, Executive Director

**The Field Foundation of
Illinois, Inc.**
135 South LaSalle Street
Suite 1250
Chicago, IL 60603
(312) 263-3211

Description: Funding for health, mental health, drug abuse programs, social services, and other concerns
Restrictions: Giving focused in Chicago, Illinois
$ Given: In FY89, 57 grants totaling $1.58 million were awarded; average range of $10,000 - $20,000 per award
Application Information: Write for application guidelines; see the important information in the chapter introduction about the need for institutional affiliation.
Deadline: None
Contact: Handy L. Lindsey, Jr., Executive Director

**Illinois Tool Works
Foundation**
8501 West Higgins Road
Chicago, IL 60631
(312) 693-3040

Description: Funding for drug abuse programs, health, hospitals, social services, and education
Restrictions: N/A
$ Given: 156 grants totaling $601,700 were awarded; range of $100 - $180,000 per award
Application Information: Write for application guidelines; see the important information in the chapter introduction about the need for institutional affiliation.
Deadline: None
Contact: Stephen B. Smith, Director

**Inland Steel-Ryerson
Foundation, Inc.**
c/o Inland Steel Industries
30 West Monroe Street
Chicago, IL 60603
(312) 899-3420

Description: Funding for human services organizations, including hospitals and facilities providing mental health services; several other funding interests
Restrictions: Giving focused in Chicago, Illinois; northwest Indiana; and areas of corporate operations
$ Given: In 1989, 181 grants totaling $1.4 million were awarded; average range of $500 - $20,000 per award
Application Information: Write for application guidelines; see the important information in the chapter introduction about the need for institutional affiliation.
Deadline: September 30
Contact: James E. Blair, Manager, Corporate Community Affairs

**John D. and Catherine T.
MacArthur Foundation**
140 S. Dearborn Street
Chicago, IL 60603
(312) 726-8000

Description: Funding for several programs, including health effort program for research in mental and behavioral health and rehabilitation
Restrictions: N/A
$ Given: Grants totaling $28.14 million were awarded
Application Information: Write for application guidelines; see the important information in the chapter introduction about the need for institutional affiliation.
Deadline: None
Contact: James M. Furman, Executive Vice President

FLOW-THROUGH FUNDING

. . . .

**Robert R. McCormick
Charitable Trust**
435 N. Michigan Avenue
Suite 770
Chicago, IL 60611
(312) 222-3510

Description: Funding for education and health services, including rehabilitation for the mentally and/or physically handicapped
Restrictions: Giving focused in Chicago, Illinois
$ Given: 427 grants were awarded; range of $500 - $4 million per award
Application Information: Write for application guidelines; see the important information in the chapter introduction about the need for institutional affiliation.
Deadlines: February 1, May 1, August 1, and December 1
Contact: Claude A. Smith, Director of Philanthropy

**Minnesota Mining and Manu-
facturing Foundation, Inc.**

For full description see listing under Minnesota

The Neisser Fund
Two North LaSalle Street
Chicago, IL 60603-3402

Description: Funding for mental health, Jewish organizations, culture, and general charitable causes
Restrictions: N/A
$ Given: In 1988, 108 grants totaling $108,500 were awarded; range of $15 - $10,000 per award
Application Information: Write for application guidelines; see the important information in the chapter introduction about the need for institutional affiliation.
Deadline: None
Contact: Edward Neisser, Director

**The Northern Trust
Company Charitable Trust**
c/o The Northern Trust
Company
50 South LaSalle Street
Chicago, IL 60675
(312) 444-3538

Description: Funding for health services, hospitals, youth, education, and community development
Restrictions: Giving focused in metropolitan Chicago, Illinois
$ Given: 645 grants totaling $1.18 million were awarded; range of $25 - $154,000 per award
Application Information: Write for application guidelines; see the important information in the chapter introduction about the need for institutional affiliation.
Deadline: February 1 for health programs
Contact: Marjorie W. Lundy, Vice President, Northern Trust Company

• • • • • • • • • • • • • • • • • • •

The Retirement Research Foundation
8765 West Higgins Road
Suite 401
Chicago, IL 60631
(312) 714-8080
FAX (312) 714-8089

Description: Special project funding for innovative programs designed to improve the quality of life of older individuals; includes support for mental health, medical research, and health/social services
Restrictions: Giving focused in the Midwestern states: Illinois, Indiana, Iowa, Kentucky, Michigan, Missouri, and Wisconsin; additional support in Florida
$ Given: In 1990, 131 grants totaling $5.6 million were awarded; average range of $30,000 - $35,000 per award
Application Information: Write for application guidelines; see the important information in the chapter introduction about the need for institutional affiliation.
Deadlines: February 1, May 1, and August 1
Contact: Marilyn Hennessy, Senior Vice President

The Seeley Foundation
115 South LaSalle Street
Room 2500
Chicago, IL 60603

Description: Research and fellowship funding in mental health fields
Restrictions: N/A
$ Given: In 1990, 6 grants totaling $201,000 were awarded; range of $4,000 - $150,000 per award
Application Information: Write for application guidelines; see the important information in the chapter introduction about the need for institutional affiliation.
Deadline: None
Contact: Hugo J. Melvoin, Secretary-Treasurer

Irvin Stern Foundation
53 West Jackson Boulevard
Suite 838
Chicago, IL 60604
(312) 786-9355

Description: Funding for Jewish organizations; support for fighting mental illness, heart disease and cancer; funding for other concerns
Restrictions: Giving focused in Chicago, Illinois; New York, New York; and San Diego, California
$ Given: In FY90, 42 grants totaling $454,700 were awarded; average range of $3,000 - $20,000 per award
Application Information: Write for application guidelines; see the important information in the chapter introduction about the need for institutional affiliation.
Deadlines: April 1 and September 1
Contact: Jeffrey Epstein, Trustee

FLOW-THROUGH FUNDING

. . . .

INDIANA

The Barker Welfare Foundation

For full description see listing under New York

Courier-Journal and Louisville Times Corporate Giving Program
525 West Broadway
Louisville, KY 40202
(502) 582-4552

Description: Funding for drug abuse programs, mental health, health, rehabilitation, family services, homelessness, and the arts
Restrictions: Giving focused in Kentucky and southern Indiana
$ Given: 41 grants totaling $610,000 were awarded; range of $500 - $158,000 per award
Application Information: Write for application guidelines; see the important information in the chapter introduction about the need for institutional affiliation.
Deadlines: January 1, May 1, and September 1
Contact: Donald Towles, Vice President, Public Affairs

Elkhart County Community Foundation, Inc.
Ameritrust National Building
301 South Main
P.O. Box 279
Elkhart, IN 46515-0279
(219) 295-8761

Description: Funding for human services, including alcohol and drug abuse programs
Restrictions: Giving restricted to Elkhart County, Indiana
$ Given: In FY90, 9 grants totaling $120,000 were awarded; range of $100 - $100,000 per award
Application Information: Write for application guidelines; see the important information in the chapter introduction about the need for institutional affiliation.
Deadlines: April 1 and October 1
Contact: William H. Myers, Executive Director

Foellinger Foundation, Inc.
520 East Berry Street
Fort Wayne, IN 46802
(219) 422-2900

Description: Funding for health and social services, including alcohol and drug abuse programs; support for education and culture
Restrictions: Giving focused in Fort Wayne, Indiana
$ Given: In FY90, 170 grants totaling $4.07 million were awarded; average range of $10,000 - $200,000 per award
Application Information: Write for application guidelines; see the important information in the chapter introduction about the need for institutional affiliation.
Deadline: 90 days before funds are needed
Contact: Harry V. Owen, President

The Indianapolis Foundation
615 North Alabama Street
Room 119
Indianapolis, IN 46204

Description: Funding for health, welfare, education, hospitals, and the handicapped
Restrictions: Giving focused in Indianapolis and Marion County, Indiana
$ Given: 84 grants totaling $2.97 million were awarded; range of $4,000 - $246,400 per award
Application Information: Write for application guidelines; see the important information in the chapter introduction about the need for institutional affiliation.
Deadlines: January 31, March 31, May 31, July 31, September 30, and November 30
Contact: Kenneth I. Chapman, Executive Director

Inland Steel-Ryerson Foundation, Inc.

For full description see listing under Illinois

The Metropolitan Health Council of Indianapolis, Inc.
401 Marott Center
342 Massachusetts Avenue
Indianapolis, IN 46204
(317) 630-1805

Description: Funding for community-based organizations providing health services, mental health services, alcohol and drug abuse programs, and dental and prenatal care
Restrictions: Giving focused in Marion County and contiguous Indiana counties
$ Given: In FY89, 30 grants totaling $847,700 were awarded; range of $2,000 - $88,700 per award
Application Information: Write for application guidelines; see the important information in the chapter introduction about the need for institutional affiliation.
Deadline: None
Contact: Betty H. Wilson, Executive Director

Minnesota Mining and Manufacturing Foundation, Inc.

For full description see listing under Minnesota

• • • • • • • • • • • • • • • • • • •

Northern Indiana Public Service Company Giving Program
5265 Hohman Avenue
Hammond, IN 64320
(219) 853-5200

Description: Funding for mental health, hospitals, health care, youth, education, and culture
Restrictions: N/A
$ Given: Grants totaling $567,000 were awarded; range of $5,000 - $10,000 per award
Application Information: Write for application guidelines; see the important information in the chapter introduction about the need for institutional affiliation.
Deadline: None
Contact: Jack W. Stine, Executive Vice President and CEO

The Retirement Research Foundation

For full description see listing under Illinois

USX Foundation, Inc.

For full description see listing under Minnesota

West Foundation, Inc.
4120 North Illinois Street
Indianapolis, IN 46208-4010
(317) 283-5525

Description: Funding for alcohol and drug abuse programs; support for international community development
Restrictions: N/A
$ Given: In 1989, grants totaling $94,700 were awarded
Application Information: Write for application guidelines; see the important information in the chapter introduction about the need for institutional affiliation.
Deadline: None
Contact: Stephen R. West, President

IOWA

The Hall Foundation, Inc.
115 Third Street, S.E.
No. 803
Cedar Rapids, IA 52401
(319) 362-9079

Description: Funding for health and social services, including mental health and drug abuse programs; support for culture, education, youth, and community development
Restrictions: Giving restricted to Cedar Rapids, Iowa
$ Given: In 1990, 47 grants totaling $3.78 million were awarded; average range of $5,000 - $50,000 per award
Application Information: Write for application guidelines; see the important information in the chapter introduction about the need for institutional affiliation.
Deadline: None
Contact: John G. Lidvall, Executive Director

• • • • • • • • • • • • • • • • • • • •

Mid-Iowa Health Foundation
550 39th Street
Suite 104
Des Moines, IA 50312
(515) 277-6411

Description: General purpose and special project funding for health services, including alcohol and drug abuse programs, mental health services, and services for the handicapped
Restrictions: Giving focused in Polk County and 7 surrounding counties of Iowa
$ Given: In 1990, 46 grants totaling $502,000 were awarded; range of $500 - $25,000 per award
Application Information: Write for application guidelines; see the important information in the chapter introduction about the need for institutional affiliation.
Deadlines: February 1, May 1, August 1, and November 1
Contact: Kathryn Bradley

Minnesota Mining and Manufacturing Foundation, Inc.

For full description see listing under Minnesota

The Retirement Research Foundation

For full description see listing under Illinois

Hobart A. and Alta V. Ross Family Foundation
P.O. Box AK
Spirit Lake, IA 51360
APPLICATION ADDRESS:
RR 9492-24
Spirit Lake, IA 51360

Description: Funding for drug and alcohol abuse programs, domestic violence and child abuse programs, youth agencies, and education
Restrictions: Giving focused in Dickinson County and surrounding counties in Iowa
$ Given: In 1989, 15 grants totaling $121,000 were awarded; range of $500 - $20,000 per award
Application Information: Write for application guidelines; see the important information in the chapter introduction about the need for institutional affiliation.
Deadline: None
Contact: Keith A. Ross, President

FLOW-THROUGH FUNDING

• •

Wahlert Foundation
c/o FDL Foods, Inc.
P.O. Box 898
Dubuque, IA 52001
(319) 588-5400

Description: Funding for health services, hospitals, drug abuse prevention programs, and several other human services
Restrictions: Giving focused in Dubuque, Iowa
$ Given: In FY90, 23 grants totaling $308,200 were awarded; average range of $100 - $35,000 per award
Application Information: Write for application guidelines; see the important information in the chapter introduction about the need for institutional affiliation.
Deadline: November 30
Contact: R.H. Wahlert, President and Treasurer

KANSAS

Louis W. & Dolpha Baehr Foundation
c/o Miami County National Bank and Trust
Box 369
Paola, KS 66071
(913) 294-4311

Description: Funding for youth programs, mental health, hospitals, education, and community development
Restrictions: Giving focused in eastern Kansas, including Kansas City
$ Given: In FY89, 13 grants totaling $178,700 were awarded; range of $600 - $75,000 per award
Application Information: Write for application guidelines; see the important information in the chapter introduction about the need for institutional affiliation.
Deadlines: March, July, September, and December
Contact: Carl F. Gump, Chairman

Topeka Community Foundation
5100 S.W. 10th
P.O. Box 4525
Topeka, KS 66604
(913) 272-4804

Description: Funding for social services, drug abuse programs, and several other concerns
Restrictions: Giving restricted to Topeka and Shawnee County, Kansas
$ Given: In 1990, 38 grants totaling $159,600 were awarded; average range of $500 - $5,000 per award
Application Information: Write for application guidelines; see the important information in the chapter introduction about the need for institutional affiliation.
Deadline: February 15
Contact: Karen Welch, Executive Director

• • • • • • • • • • • • • • • • • • •

KENTUCKY

**Courier-Journal and
Louisville Times Corporate
Giving Program**

For full description see listing under Indiana

The Gheens Foundation, Inc.
One Riverfront Plaza
Suite 705
Louisville, KY 40202
(502) 584-4650
FAX (502) 584-4652

Description: Special project funding for health and social
service agencies, programs for the mentally and/or physically
handicapped, education, and culture
Restrictions: Giving in Kentucky, with focus on Louisville
$ Given: In FY90, 41 grants totaling $1.55 million were
awarded; average range of $10,000 - $50,000 per award
Application Information: Write for application guidelines;
see the important information in the chapter introduction
about the need for institutional affiliation.
Deadline: None
Contact: James N. Davis, Executive Director

**Minnesota Mining and Manu-
facturing Foundation, Inc.**

For full description see listing under Minnesota

**The Retirement Research
Foundation**

For full description see listing under Illinois

LOUISIANA

**Fred B. and Ruth B. Zigler
Foundation**
P.O. Box 986
Jennings, LA 70546
(318) 824-2413

Description: Funding for drug abuse programs, education,
youth agencies, and a museum
Restrictions: Giving focused in Jefferson Davis Parish, Louisiana
$ Given: In 1989, 35 grants totaling $159,000 were awarded;
range of $75 - $45,000 per award
Application Information: Write for application guidelines;
see the important information in the chapter introduction
about the need for institutional affiliation.
Deadline: Bimonthly
Contact: Margaret Cormier, Secretary-Treasurer

FLOW-THROUGH FUNDING

● ● ● ● ● ● ● ● ● ● ● ● ● ● ● ● ● ● ● ●

MAINE

The Maine Community Foundation, Inc.
210 Main Street
P.O. Box 148
Ellsworth, ME 04605
(207) 667-9735

Description: Funding for alcoholism, as well as for education, welfare, arts, and the environment
Restrictions: Giving strictly limited to Maine
$ Given: In 1990, 234 grants totaling $560,000 were awarded; average range of $500 - $5,000 per award
Application Information: Write for application guidelines; see the important information in the chapter introduction about the need for institutional affiliation.
Deadlines: February 1, April 1, August 1, and October 1
Contact: Rebecca Buyers-Baso, Program Director

MARYLAND

Charles S. Abell Foundation, Inc.
8401 Connecticut Avenue
Chevy Chase, MD 20815
(301) 652-2224

Description: Funding for the mentally handicapped, as well as for church-related centers and services for abused women and children
Restrictions: Giving focused in Washington, DC and five nearby Maryland counties
$ Given: In 1990, 16 grants totaling $222,000 were awarded; range of $1,000 - $50,000 per award
Application Information: Write for application guidelines; see the important information in the chapter introduction about the need for institutional affiliation.
Deadline: None
Contact: W. Shepherdson Abell, Secretary-Treasurer

Community Foundation of the Eastern Shore, Inc.
One Plaza East
Suite 526-528
Salisbury, MD 21801
(301) 742-9911
ADDITIONAL ADDRESS:
P.O. Box 156
Salisbury, MD 21803

Description: Funding for human services, including drug abuse programs; support for health services and hospitals
Restrictions: Giving limited to the area within a 50-mile radius of Salisbury, Maryland
$ Given: In FY90, 4,000 grants totaling $390,000 were awarded; range of $100 - $5,000 per award
Application Information: Write for application guidelines; see the important information in the chapter introduction about the need for institutional affiliation.
Deadlines: 60 days prior to board meetings; board meets in February, June, and October
Contact: Lucy A. Mohler, Executive Director

Giant Food Foundation, Inc.	**For full description see listing under District of Columbia**
Heileman Old Style Foundation, Inc.	**For full description see listing under Wisconsin**

The Marion I. and Henry J. Knott Foundation, Inc.
3904 Hickory Avenue
Baltimore, MD 21211
(301) 235-7068

Description: Funding for Roman Catholic activities and other human services; support for programs for the mentally ill; several other areas of funding interest
Restrictions: Giving restricted to the area of Maryland served by the Archdiocese of Baltimore (all counties except those south of Frederick, Anne Arundel, and Howard, and the Eastern Shore region)
$ Given: In 1990, 38 grants totaling $909,000 were awarded; average range of $10,000 - $30,000 per award
Application Information: Write for application guidelines; see the important information in the chapter introduction about the need for institutional affiliation.
Deadlines: February 1 and August 1
Contact: Ann von Lossberg, Executive Director

Little River Foundation
Whitewood Farm
The Plains, VA 22171
(703) 253-5540

Description: Funding for hospitals, drug abuse programs, and AIDS programs; additional support for education, the environment, religion, and community funds
Restrictions: Giving focused in the mid-Atlantic states
$ Given: In FY90, 44 grants totaling $302,000 were awarded; average range of $500 - $100,000 per award
Application Information: Write for application guidelines; see the important information in the chapter introduction about the need for institutional affiliation.
Deadline: None
Contact: Dale D. Hogoboom, Assistant Treasurer

Eugene and Agnes E. Meyer Foundation	**For full description see listing under District of Columbia**

FLOW-THROUGH FUNDING

• • • • • • • • • • • • • • • • • • •

Nathan Foundation, Inc.
c/o Mercantile-Safe Deposit
& Trust Co.
766 Old Hammonds Ferry Road
Linthicum, MD 21090
APPLICATION ADDRESS:
c/o Mercantile-Safe Deposit &
Trust Co., Two Hopkins Plaza
Baltimore, MD 21201
(301) 237-5518

Description: Funding for the mentally and physically handicapped, as well as for the indigent
Restrictions: Giving strictly limited to Dorchester County, MD
$ Given: In 1990, 34 grants totaling $176,000 were awarded; range of $250 - $40,000 per award
Application Information: Write for application guidelines; see the important information in the chapter introduction about the need for institutional affiliation.
Deadline: None
Contact: Paul P. Klender, Treasurer

van Ameringen Foundation, Inc.

For full description see listing under New York

MASSACHUSETTS

The Frank Stanley Beveridge Foundation, Inc.
301 Yamato Road
Suite 1130
Boca Raton, FL 33431-4929
(407) 241-8388
(800) 356-9779
FAX (407) 241-8332

Description: Funding for a local park, and for health and social services, including mental health programs
Restrictions: Giving focused in Hampden County, Massachusetts
$ Given: In 1990, 91 grants totaling $1.92 million were awarded; average range of $1,000 - $25,000 per award
Application Information: Write for application guidelines; see the important information in the chapter introduction about the need for institutional affiliation.
Deadlines: February 1 and August 1
Contact: Philip Caswell, President

Cambridge Community Foundation
99 Bishop Allen Drive
Cambridge, MA 02139
(617) 876-5214

Description: General purpose and special project funding in four areas: (1) social services; (2) education; (3) health, including mental health and substance abuse programs; and (4) shelter
Restrictions: Giving is focused in Cambridge, Massachusetts, unless specified otherwise by the donor
$ Given: In 1988, grants totaling $181,000 were awarded; range of $1,000 - $5,000 per award
Application Information: Write for application guidelines; see the important information in the chapter introduction about the need for institutional affiliation.
Deadlines: April 15 and October 15
Contact: Lynn D'Ambrose, Executive Director

• • • • • • • • • • • • • • • • • • • •

The Fred Harris Daniels Foundation, Inc.
c/o The Mechanics Bank
Trust Department
P.O. Box 987
Worcester, MA 01613
(508) 798-6443
APPLICATION ADDRESS:
c/o The Mechanics Bank,
Trust Department
2000 Mechanics Tower
Worcester, MA 01608

Description: Funding for health services, including programs for the mentally ill; support for sciences, social services, education, and culture
Restrictions: Giving focused in the Worcester, Massachusetts area
$ Given: In FY90, 71 grants totaling $451,300 were awarded; average range of $1,000 - $20,000 per award
Application Information: Write for application guidelines; see the important information in the chapter introduction about the need for institutional affiliation.
Deadlines: March 1, June 1, September 1, and December 1
Contact: Bruce G. Daniels, President

Eugene A. Dexter Charitable Fund
c/o Bay Bank Valley Trust Co.
P.O. Box 3422
Burlington, MA 01803
(617) 273-1700

Description: Funding for health and welfare, with emphasis on the mentally and physically handicapped, as well as on minorities and children
Restrictions: Giving focused in Hampden County, Massachusetts, with preference for the Springfield area
$ Given: In 1990, grants totaling $601,000 were awarded
Application Information: Write for application guidelines; see the important information in the chapter introduction about the need for institutional affiliation.
Deadline: None
Contact: Bernie Stephan, Trust Officer, BayBank Valley Trust Co.

Harry Doehla Foundation, Inc.
c/o Singer and Lusardi
370 Main Street
Worcester, MA 01608
(508) 756-4657

Description: Funding for health organizations, including those addressing mental health
Restrictions: N/A
$ Given: In FY89, 18 grants totaling $174,000 were awarded; range of $500 - $35,000 per award
Application Information: Write for application guidelines; see the important information in the chapter introduction about the need for institutional affiliation.
Deadline: None
Contact: Henry Lusardi, President

The Fuller Foundation, Inc.   **For full description see listing in New Hampshire**

FLOW-THROUGH FUNDING

• • • • • • • • • • • • • • • • • • •

The Hyams Foundation
One Boston Place
32nd Floor
Boston, MA 02108
(617) 720-2238
FAX (617) 720-2434

Description: General purpose and special project funding for social services, including mental health counseling, substance abuse programs, health services, and urban youth programs
Restrictions: Giving focused in Boston, Cambridge, Chelsea, Lynn, and Somerville, Massachusetts
$ Given: In 1990, 224 grants totaling $3.25 million were awarded; average range of $15,000 - $25,000 per award
Application Information: Write for application guidelines; see the important information in the chapter introduction about the need for institutional affiliation.
Deadline: None
Contact: Elizabeth B. Smith, Executive Director

Edward Bangs Kelley and Elza Kelley Foundation, Inc.
243 South Street
P.O. Drawer M
Hyannis, MA 02601
(508) 775-3117

Description: Funding for local health and welfare programs, including drug and alcohol abuse programs, health services, and hospitals
Restrictions: Giving strictly limited to Barnstable County, Massachusetts
$ Given: In 1989, 27 grants totaling $116,000 were awarded; range of $150 - $17,000 per award
Application Information: Write for application guidelines; see the important information in the chapter introduction about the need for institutional affiliation.
Deadline: None
Contact: Henry L. Murphy, Administrative Manager

Minnesota Mining and Manufacturing Foundation, Inc.

For full description see listing under Minnesota

Poitras Charitable Foundation, Inc.
198 Highland Street
Holliston, MA 01746

Description: Funding for mental health, hospitals, medical research, social services, and conservation
Restrictions: Giving focused in Massachusetts
$ Given: In 1989, 11 grants totaling $184,000 were awarded; range of $500 - $115,000 per award
Application Information: Write for application guidelines; see the important information in the chapter introduction about the need for institutional affiliation.
Deadline: N/A
Contact: Patricia T. Poitras, President

• • • • • • • • • • • • • • • • • • • •

van Ameringen Foundation, Inc.

For full description see listing under New York

MICHIGAN

Dorothy U. Dalton Foundation, Inc.
c/o Old Kent Bank of Kalamazoo
151 East Michigan Avenue
Kalamazoo, MI 49007
(616) 383-6958

Description: Funding for mental health, social services, education, youth agencies, and cultural programs
Restrictions: Giving focused in Kalamazoo County, Michigan
$ Given: In 1989, 78 grants totaling $1.27 million were awarded; range of $100 - $100,000 per award
Application Information: Write for application guidelines; see the important information in the chapter introduction about the need for institutional affiliation.
Deadlines: Proposals accepted in April and October
Contact: Ronald N. Kilgore, Secretary-Treasurer

J.F. Ervin Foundation
3893 Research Park Drive
P.O. Box 1168
Ann Arbor, MI 48106
(313) 769-4600

Description: Funding for health services, hospitals, drug abuse programs, and other human services
Restrictions: Giving focused in southeastern Michigan
$ Given: In 1990, 38 grants totaling $77,000 were awarded; range of $150 - $6,500 per award
Application Information: Write for application guidelines; see the important information in the chapter introduction about the need for institutional affiliation.
Deadline: None
Contact: Harriet A. Birch, Secretary

Heileman Old Style Foundation, Inc.

For full description see listing under Wisconsin

Hexcel Foundation

For full description see listing under California

FLOW-THROUGH FUNDING

• • • • • • • • • • • • • • • • • • • •

The Jackson Community Foundation
230 West Michigan Avenue
Jackson, MI 49201-2230
(517) 787-1321

Description: Funding for community improvement efforts, including drug abuse programs, health services, and family services
Restrictions: Giving strictly limited to Jackson County, Michigan
$ Given: In 1989, 20 grants totaling $286,000 were awarded; average range of $500 - $18,000 per award
Application Information: Write for application guidelines; see the important information in the chapter introduction about the need for institutional affiliation.
Deadlines: February 1, May 1, August 1, and November 1
Contact: Mrs. Jody Bacon, Executive Director

Elizabeth E. Kennedy Fund
500 City Center Building
Ann Arbor, MI 48104
(313) 761-3780

Description: Seed money and some other forms of funding for mental health, health, medical research, education, the arts, and the environment
Restrictions: Giving focused in Michigan, with preference for less populated regions
$ Given: In 1989, 12 grants totaling $118,000 were awarded; average range of $1,000 - $10,000 per award
Application Information: Write for application guidelines; see the important information in the chapter introduction about the need for institutional affiliation.
Deadline: None
Contact: John S. Dobson, Secretary

Minnesota Mining and Manufacturing Foundation, Inc.

For full description see listing under Minnesota

The Retirement Research Foundation

For full description see listing under Illinois

• • • • • • • • • • • • • • • • • • •

The Skillman Foundation
333 West Fort Street
Suite 1350
Detroit, MI 48226
(313) 961-8850

Description: Funding for organizations addressing the needs of the young and the elderly (especially the disadvantaged) in southeastern Mighigan; support for drug abuse programs, social services, family services, welfare, etc.
Restrictions: Giving focused in southeastern Michigan, with emphasis on the Detroit area, including Wayne, Macomb, and Oakland counties
$ Given: In 1990, 162 grants totaling $12.56 million were awarded; average range of $20,000 - $100,000 per award
Application Information: Write for application guidelines; see the important information in the chapter introduction about the need for institutional affiliation.
Deadline: None
Contact: John F. Ziraldo, Program Officer

Young Woman's Home Association of Detroit
1233 Audubon Road
Grosse Pointe Park, MI 48230
(313) 886-6970
APPLICATION ADDRESS:
Mrs. Thomas Cracchiolo
561 Lakeshore Road
Grosse Pointe Shores, MI 48236

Description: Funding for health associations and drug abuse programs, hospitals and social services, and other human services
Restrictions: Giving focused in Detroit, Michigan
$ Given: In FY91, 40 grants totaling $59,000 were awarded; range of $25 - $4,000 per award
Application Information: Write for application guidelines; see the important information in the chapter introduction about the need for institutional affiliation.
Deadline: September 1
Contact: Mrs. John Young

MINNESOTA

Patrick and Aimee Butler Family Foundation
First National Bank Building
332 Minnesota Street
E-1420
St. Paul, MN 55101-1369
(612) 222-2565

Description: Funding for chemical dependency programs, Catholic institutions, education, the arts, and human services
Restrictions: Giving focused in St. Paul and Minneapolis, Minnesota; no support for health care, hospitals, or medical research
$ Given: In 1990, 102 grants totaling $871,000 were awarded; range of $500 - $200,000 per award
Application Information: Write for application guidelines; see the important information in the chapter introduction about the need for institutional affiliation.
Deadline: May 1
Contact: Sandra K. Butler, Program Officer

FLOW-THROUGH FUNDING

. . . .

Edwin W. and Catherine M. Davis Foundation
2100 First National Bank Building
St. Paul, MN 55101
(612) 228-0935

Description: Funding for mental health, social welfare, education, the arts, and the environment
Restrictions: N/A
$ Given: In 1990, 64 grants totaling $630,000 were awarded; average range of $5,000 - $20,000 per award
Application Information: Write for application guidelines; see the important information in the chapter introduction about the need for institutional affiliation.
Deadline: None
Contact: Bette D. Moorman, President

Heileman Old Style Foundation, Inc.

For full description see listing under Wisconsin

Minnesota Mining and Manufacturing Foundation, Inc.
3M Center
Building 521-11-01
St. Paul, MN 55144-1000
(612) 736-3781

Description: Funding for human services, including programs for alcohol and drug abuse; support for education, the arts, preventive health care, and community funds
Restrictions: Giving focused in areas with corporate facilities, including areas in Alabama, California, Georgia, Illinois, Indiana, Iowa, Kentucky, Massachusetts, Michigan, Minnesota, Mississippi, Missouri, Nebraska, New Jersey, North Carolina, North Dakota, Ohio, Oklahoma, Oregon, Pennsylvania, South Carolina, South Dakota, Texas, Utah, Virginia, Washington, West Virginia, and Wisconsin
$ Given: In 1989, grants totaling $8.5 million were awarded; average range of $500 - $25,000 per award
Application Information: Write for application guidelines; see the important information in the chapter introduction about the need for institutional affiliation.
Deadlines: 8 weeks prior to board meetings; board meets in March, August, and December
Contact: Eugene W. Steele, Secretary

• • • • • • • • • • • • • • • • • • • •

Ordean Foundation
501 Ordean Building
424 West Superior Street
Duluth, MN 55802
(218) 726-4785

Description: Funding for drug and alcohol programs, mental illness institutions, and other health and youth activities; support for local relief efforts
Restrictions: Giving restricted to Duluth and contiguous cities in St. Louis County, Minnesota; no support for national campaigns
$ Given: In 1990, 62 grants totaling $896,000 were awarded; average range of $100 - $166,500 per award
Application Information: Write for application guidelines; see the important information in the chapter introduction about the need for institutional affiliation.
Deadline: 15th of each month
Contact: Antoinette Poupore-Haats, Executive Director

Alex Stern Family Foundation

For full description see listing under North Dakota

USX Foundation, Inc.
600 Grant Street
Room 2640
Pittsburgh, PA 15219-4776
(412) 433-5237

Description: General purpose, research, and capital funding for health and medicine, including mental health; many other areas of interest, ranging from education to civic affairs and social services
Restrictions: Giving focused mainly in areas of corporate operations, including Pittsburgh and Bucks County, Pennsylvania; Birmingham, Alabama; Gary, Indiana; and northeastern Minnesota
$ Given: In FY89, 168 grants totaling $5.3 million were awarded
Application Information: Write for application guidelines; see the important information in the chapter introduction about the need for institutional affiliation.
Deadline: Health and medical services deadline, July 15
Contact: James L. Hamilton III, General Manager

Archie D. and Bertha H. Walker Foundation
1121 Hennepin Avenue
Minneapolis, MN 55403
(612) 332-3556

Description: Funding for chemical dependency programs (especially alcoholism); grants to combat racism
Restrictions: Giving focused in the seven-county area of metropolitan Minneapolis-St. Paul, Minnesota
$ Given: In 1990, 53 grants totaling $492,000 were awarded; range of $1,000 - $120,000 per award
Application Information: Write for application guidelines; see the important information in the chapter introduction about the need for institutional affiliation.
Deadline: December 1
Contact: David H. Griffith, President

FLOW-THROUGH FUNDING

. . . .

The Wasie Foundation
909 Foshay Tower
Minneapolis, MN 55402
(612) 332-3883

Description: Funding for health organizations, mental health, family issues, education, and Roman Catholic religious associations
Restrictions: Giving strictly limited to the metropolitan Minneapolis-St. Paul, Minnesota area
$ Given: In 1989, 48 grants totaling $276,500 were awarded; average range of $3,000 - $5,000 per award
Application Information: Write for application guidelines; see the important information in the chapter introduction about the need for institutional affiliation.
Deadline: Varies
Contact: Gregg D. Sjoquist, Executive Director

Wedum Foundation
6860 Flying Cloud Drive
Eden Prairie, MN 55344
(612) 944-5547

Description: Funding for social services, alcoholism, health associations, education, and the environment
Restrictions: Giving focused in the area of Alexandria, Minnesota
$ Given: In 1989, 28 grants totaling $275,000 were awarded; range of $50 - $100,000 per award
Application Information: Write for application guidelines; see the important information in the chapter introduction about the need for institutional affiliation.
Deadline: None
Contact: Mayo Johnson, President

Whitney Foundation
1900 Foshay Tower
821 Marquette Avenue
Minneapolis, MN 55402

Description: Funding for social services, alcoholism, drug abuse, child/youth welfare, AIDS, education, and the arts
Restrictions: Giving strictly limited to Minnesota, with emphasis on Ramsey and Hennepin counties
$ Given: In 1990, 250 grants totaling $252,400 were awarded; average range of $200 - $1,000 per award
Application Information: Write for application guidelines; see the important information in the chapter introduction about the need for institutional affiliation.
Deadline: Varies
Contact: Gladys Green

• • • • • • • • • • • • • • • • • • •

MISSISSIPPI

Minnesota Mining and Manufacturing Foundation, Inc.
3M Center
Building 521-11-01
St. Paul, MN 55144-1000
(612) 736-3781

Description: Funding for human services, including programs for alcohol and drug abuse; support for education, the arts, preventive health care, and community funds
Restrictions: Giving focused in areas with corporate facilities, including areas in Alabama, California, Georgia, Illinois, Indiana, Iowa, Kentucky, Massachusetts, Michigan, Minnesota, Mississippi, Missouri, Nebraska, New Jersey, North Carolina, North Dakota, Ohio, Oklahoma, Oregon, Pennsylvania, South Carolina, South Dakota, Texas, Utah, Virginia, Washington, West Virginia, and Wisconsin
$ Given: In 1989, grants totaling $8.5 million were awarded; average range of $500 - $25,000 per award
Application Information: Write for application guidelines; see the important information in the chapter introduction about the need for institutional affiliation.
Deadlines: 8 weeks prior to board meetings; board meets in March, August, and December
Contact: Eugene W. Steele, Secretary

MISSOURI

Community Foundation, Inc.
901 St. Louis Street
Suite 303
Springfield, MO 65806
(417) 864-6199

Description: Seed money and matching funds for health, social services, alcohol abuse prevention, education, youth projects, and the arts
Restrictions: Giving focused in southwest Missouri
$ Given: In FY90, grants totaling $73,000 were awarded
Application Information: Write for application guidelines; see the important information in the chapter introduction about the need for institutional affiliation.
Deadlines: March and September
Contact: Jan Horton, Executive Director

FLOW-THROUGH FUNDING

• • • • • • • • • • • • • • • • • • •

Milton W. Feld Charitable Trust
2345 Grand Avenue
Suite 2800
Kansas City, MO 64108
(816) 474-6460

Description: Funding for social services, including drug abuse programs; support for hospitals and medical research; funding for education, welfare, and culture
Restrictions: Giving focused in Kansas City and St. Louis, Missouri
$ Given: In FY90, 38 grants totaling $328,000 were awarded; average range of $1,000 - $50,000 per award
Application Information: Write for application guidelines; see the important information in the chapter introduction about the need for institutional affiliation.
Deadline: None
Contact: Abraham E. Margolin, Trustee

Minnesota Mining and Manufacturing Foundation, Inc.

For full description see listing under Minnesota

Oppenstein Brothers Foundation
911 Main Street
Suite 100
P.O. Box 13095
Kansas City, MO 64199-3095
(816) 234-8671

Description: Funding for social services, including programs for the mentally ill; grants for education, preventive health care, and welfare
Restrictions: Giving focused in the metropolitan Kansas City, Missouri area
$ Given: In FY91, 74 grants totaling $830,000 were awarded; range of $1,000 - $80,000 per award
Application Information: Write for application guidelines; see the important information in the chapter introduction about the need for institutional affiliation.
Deadline: Varies
Contact: Candace L. Fowler, Program Officer

Pitzman Fund
c/o Boatmen's Trust Co.
100 North Broadway
P.O. Box 14737
St. Louis, MO 63178
(314) 436-9042

Description: General purpose funding for drug abuse programs, social services, and other human services
Restrictions: Giving focused in St. Louis, Missouri
$ Given: In FY90, 27 grants totaling $54,500 were awarded; average range of $500 - $1,500 per award
Application Information: Write for application guidelines; see the important information in the chapter introduction about the need for institutional affiliation.
Deadline: None
Contact: Roy T. Blair, Trust Officer

• • • • • • • • • • • • • • • • • • • •

The Retirement Research Foundation

For full description see listing under Illinois

Joseph H. and Florence A. Roblee Foundation
c/o Boatmen's Trust Co.
510 Locust Street
P.O. Box 14737
St. Louis, MO 63178

Description: Funding for mental health, social problems, education, and religion
Restrictions: Giving focused mainly in California, Florida, Missouri, New York, North Carolina, and Texas
$ Given: In 1988, 90 grants totaling $367,000 were awarded; average range of $500 - $15,000 per award
Application Information: Write for application guidelines; see the important information in the chapter introduction about the need for institutional affiliation.
Deadlines: March 15 and September 1
Contact: Carol M. Duhme, President; or Roy T. Blair, Trust Officer

Victor E. Speas Foundation
c/o Boatmen's First National
Bank of Kansas City
14 West Tenth Street
Kansas City, MO 64183
(816) 691-7481

Description: Funding for health care improvement, including support for organizations addressing alcoholism, drug abuse, and mental illness
Restrictions: Giving focused in Jackson, Clay, Platte, and Cass counties, Missouri
$ Given: In 1989, 38 grants totaling $1.26 million were awarded; average range of $5,000 - $50,000 per award
Application Information: Write for application guidelines; see the important information in the chapter introduction about the need for institutional affiliation.
Deadline: None
Contact: David P. Ross, Senior Vice President, Boatmen's First National Bank of Kansas City

John W. and Effie E. Speas Memorial Trust
c/o Boatmen's First National
Bank of Kansas City
14 West Tenth Street
Kansas City, MO 64183
(816) 691-7481
APPLICATION ADDRESS:
Boatmen's First National
Bank of Kansas City
P.O. Box 419038
Kansas City, MO 64183

Description: Funding for hospitals and health services, as well as support for the mentally disabled; funding for medical education and research
Restrictions: Giving focused in the metropolitan Kansas City area
$ Given: In 1989, 28 grants totaling $1.2 million were awarded; average range of $5,000 - $100,000 per award
Application Information: Write for application guidelines; see the important information in the chapter introduction about the need for institutional affiliation.
Deadline: None
Contact: David P. Ross, Senior Vice President, Boatmen's First National Bank of Kansas City

FLOW-THROUGH FUNDING

• • • • • • • • • • • • • • • • • • • •

Edward F. Swinney Trust
c/o Boatmen's First National
Bank of Kansas City
P.O. Box 419038
Kansas City, MO 64183
APPLICATION ADDRESS:
c/o Kansas City Community
Foundation
406 Board of Trade Building
Tenth and Wyandotte Sts.
Kansas City, MO 64105
(816) 842-0944

Description: Funding for mental health, hospitals, rehabilitation, and other human services
Restrictions: Giving restricted to Kansas City, Missouri
$ Given: In 1988, 23 grants totaling $474,000 were awarded; range of $2,500 - $100,000 per award
Application Information: Write for application guidelines; see the important information in the chapter introduction about the need for institutional affiliation.
Deadlines: February 3, June 1, August 31, and November 3
Contact: Dalene Bradford, Vice President, Programs; or Terry Henrichs, Program Secretary

NEBRASKA

Minnesota Mining and Manufacturing Foundation, Inc.
3M Center
Building 521-11-01
St. Paul, MN 55144-1000
(612) 736-3781

Description: Funding for human services, including programs for alcohol and drug abuse; support for education, the arts, preventive health care, and community funds
Restrictions: Giving focused in areas with corporate facilities, including areas in Alabama, California, Georgia, Illinois, Indiana, Iowa, Kentucky, Massachusetts, Michigan, Minnesota, Mississippi, Missouri, Nebraska, New Jersey, North Carolina, North Dakota, Ohio, Oklahoma, Oregon, Pennsylvania, South Carolina, South Dakota, Texas, Utah, Virginia, Washington, West Virginia, and Wisconsin
$ Given: In 1989, grants totaling $8.5 million were awarded; average range of $500 - $25,000 per award
Application Information: Write for application guidelines; see the important information in the chapter introduction about the need for institutional affiliation.
Deadlines: 8 weeks prior to board meetings; board meets in March, August, and December
Contact: Eugene W. Steele, Secretary

• •

NEVADA

Hexcel Foundation
P.O. Box 2312
Dublin, CA 94568
(415) 828-4200

Description: Funding for mental health and drug abuse treatment centers; support for health, welfare, youth, culture, and community projects
Restrictions: Giving in San Francisco, Dublin, Pleasanton, Livermore, City of Industry, Chatsworth, and San Diego, California; support also in areas of Arizona, Michigan, Nevada, Ohio, Pennsylvania, and Texas
$ Given: 42 grants totaling $104,800 were awarded; range of $125 - $25,800 per award
Application Information: Write for application guidelines; see the important information in the chapter introduction about the need for institutional affiliation.
Deadline: None
Contact: Karel Kramer Marriott, Manager of Corporate Contributions

Pacific Telesis Foundation

For full description see listing under California

NEW HAMPSHIRE

The Fuller Foundation, Inc.
Box 461
Rye Beach, NH 03871
(603) 964-6998

Description: Funding for drug abuse programs, education, and medical research
Restrictions: Giving focused in Boston, Massachusetts and the New Hampshire seacoast area
$ Given: In 1990, 95 grants totaling $296,000 were awarded; average range of $1,000 - $5,000 per award
Application Information: Write for application guidelines; see the important information in the chapter introduction about the need for institutional affiliation.
Deadlines: March 15, August 15, and December 15
Contact: John T. Bottomley, Executive Director

FLOW-THROUGH FUNDING

• •

NEW JERSEY

Emil Buehler Foundation, Inc.
60 Route 17 South
Paramus, NJ 07652
(201) 843-1333

Description: Funding for biochemical research for a mental health program; support for aviation promotion
Restrictions: Giving focused in Florida and New Jersey
$ Given: In FY90, 9 grants totaling $117,000 were awarded; range of $5,000 - $25,000 per award
Application Information: Write for application guidelines; see the important information in the chapter introduction about the need for institutional affiliation.
Deadline: None
Contact: Grant Administrator

The Frances L. & Edwin L. Cummings Memorial Fund
501 Fifth Avenue
Suite 1208
New York, NY 10017-1602
(212) 286-1778

Description: Funding for several medical and health/welfare concerns, including education and rehabilitation of the physically and/or mentally handicapped
Restrictions: Giving focused in metropolitan New York, including Connecticut and New Jersey
$ Given: In FY90, 48 grants totaling $1.4 million were awarded; average range of $10,000 - $25,000 per award
Application Information: Write for application guidelines; see the important information in the chapter introduction about the need for institutional affiliation.
Deadlines: April 1 and October 1
Contact: Elizabeth Costas, Administrative Director

The Freed Foundation, Inc.

For full description see listing under District of Columbia

The Robert Wood Johnson Foundation
P.O. Box 2316
Princeton, NJ 08543-2316
(609) 452-8701

Description: Seed money and research and special project funding for health care improvement, including support for substance abuse programs
Restrictions: Giving only to organizations and activities within the United States; no support for disease-specific institutions/programs
$ Given: In 1990, grants totaling $109 million were awarded; average range of $55,000 - $200,000 per award
Application Information: Write for application guidelines; see the important information in the chapter introduction about the need for institutional affiliation.
Deadline: None
Contact: Edward H. Robbins, Proposal Manager

. . . .

The Joe and Emily Lowe Foundation, Inc.

For full description see listing under Florida

The Curtis W. McGraw Foundation
c/o Drinker, Biddle & Reath
P.O. Box 627
Princeton, NJ 08542
(609) 497-7011

Description: Funding for mental health, hospitals, social services, AIDS research, and education
Restrictions: Giving focused in Princeton, New Jersey; Vail, Colorado; and Sun Valley, Idaho
$ Given: In 1990, 66 grants totaling $591,000 were awarded; range of $1,000 - $61,000 per award
Application Information: Write for application guidelines; see the important information in the chapter introduction about the need for institutional affiliation.
Deadline: October 15
Contact: Samuel W. Lambert III, Secretary-Treasurer

Minnesota Mining and Manufacturing Foundation, Inc.

For full description see listing under Minnesota

Mutual of New York Foundation

For full description see listing under New York

The Schultz Foundation
1037 Route 46 East
Suite 207
Clifton, NJ 07013
(201) 614-8880

Description: Funding for medical research, drug abuse programs, and hospices
Restrictions: Giving focused mainly in north central New Jersey
$ Given: In FY90, 39 grants totaling $664,000 were awarded; average range of $100 - $151,000 per award
Application Information: Write for application guidelines; see the important information in the chapter introduction about the need for institutional affiliation.
Deadline: None
Contact: William L.S. Rigg, Executive Director

FLOW-THROUGH FUNDING

• • • • • • • • • • • • • • • • • • • •

Ann Earle Talcott Fund
c/o First Fidelity Bank, N.A., NJ
Philanthropic Services Group
765 Broad Street
Newark, NJ 07102
(201) 430-4533

Description: Seed money and special project funding for human services, including activities for the mentally ill; additional support for education and animal welfare
Restrictions: Giving focused in New Jersey
$ Given: In FY90, 9 grants totaling $67,500 were awarded; average range of $1,000 - $25,000 per award
Application Information: Write for application guidelines; see the important information in the chapter introduction about the need for institutional affiliation.
Deadlines: February 1 and August 1
Contact: James S. Hohn, Assistant Vice President, First Fidelity Bank, N.A., NJ

Victoria Foundation, Inc.
40 South Fullerton Avenue
Montclair, NJ 07042
(201) 783-4450

Description: Funding for urban improvement activities, including substance abuse programs; support for youth agencies and the environment
Restrictions: Giving focused in Greater Newark, New Jersey
$ Given: In 1990, 117 grants totaling $4 million were awarded; average range of $20,000 - $50,000 per award
Application Information: Write for application guidelines; see the important information in the chapter introduction about the need for institutional affiliation.
Deadlines: February 1 and September 1
Contact: Catherine M. McFarland, Executive Officer

Windie Foundation
c/o Drinker Biddle & Reath
P.O. Box 627
Princeton, NJ 08542-3712
(609) 921-6336

Description: Ongoing funding for resident homes assisting female alcoholics; support for the environment
Restrictions: Giving focused in New Jersey
$ Given: In 1989, 1 grant for $65,000 was awarded
Application Information: Write for application guidelines; see the important information in the chapter introduction about the need for institutional affiliation.
Deadline: None
Contact: Samuel W. Lambert III, Trustee

NEW MEXICO

J.F. Maddox Foundation
P.O. Box 5410
Hobbs, NM 88241
(505) 393-6338

Description: Funding for self-help projects, including drug abuse programs; support for education, the arts, and the elderly
Restrictions: Giving focused in New Mexico and western Texas
$ Given: In FY90, 77 grants totaling $1.95 million were awarded; average range of $1,000 - $25,000 per award
Application Information: Write for application guidelines; see the important information in the chapter introduction about the need for institutional affiliation.
Deadline: None
Contact: Robert D. Socolofsky, Executive Director

NEW YORK

The Achelis Foundation
c/o Morris & McVeigh
767 Third Avenue
New York, NY 10017
(212) 418-0588

Description: Funding for social services and health care, including hospitals, drug abuse programs, and medical research
Restrictions: Giving focused in New York
$ Given: In 1990, 35 grants totaling $800,000 were awarded; average range of $10,000 - $30,000 per award
Application Information: Write for application guidelines; see the important information in the chapter introduction about the need for institutional affiliation.
Deadline: None
Contact: Mary E. Caslin, Secretary and Executive Director

American Chai Trust
c/o Bernard Perlman
470 Park Avenue South
12th Floor
New York, NY 10016
(212) 889-0575

Description: Seed money and special project funding for human services and health, including programs on mental health, drug abuse, and alcoholism
Restrictions: N/A
$ Given: In FY90, grants totaling $50,700 were awarded; average range of $2,000 - $5,000 per award
Application Information: Write for application guidelines; see the important information in the chapter introduction about the need for institutional affiliation.
Deadline: None

FLOW-THROUGH FUNDING

. . . .

Rose M. Badgeley Residuary Charitable Trust
c/o Marine Midland Bank, N.A.
250 Park Avenue
New York, NY 10177
(212) 503-2773

Description: Funding for health associations and social services, including alcoholism programs; support for medical research, education, hospitals, youth, and culture
Restrictions: Giving focused mainly in metropolitan New York, New York
$ Given: In FY91, 16 grants totaling $631,500 were awarded; average range of $5,000 - $25,000 per award
Application Information: Write for application guidelines; see the important information in the chapter introduction about the need for institutional affiliation.
Deadline: Proposals accepted December 1 through March 15
Contact: Mr. Loren R. Sattinger, Vice President, Marine Midland Bank, N.A.

The Baird Foundation
P.O. Box 514
Williamsville, NY 14221
(716) 633-5588

Description: General purpose funding for alcoholism programs, social services, medical research, education, the arts, and other concerns
Restrictions: Giving focused in Erie County, New York
$ Given: In 1990, 109 grants totaling $358,500 were awarded; average range of $1,000 - $2,000 per award
Application Information: Write for application guidelines; see the important information in the chapter introduction about the need for institutional affiliation.
Deadline: Proposals accepted January 1 through May 21
Contact: Carl E. Gruber, Manager

Banbury Fund, Inc.
c/o Tardino & Stewart
101 Park Avenue
35th Floor
New York, NY 10178

Description: Funding for health and welfare agencies, including programs for alcoholism; support for scientific research and education
Restrictions: Giving focused in New York
$ Given: In 1989, grants totaling $975,000 were awarded; average range of $3,000 - $15,000 per award
Application Information: Write for application guidelines; see the important information in the chapter introduction about the need for institutional affiliation.
Deadline: None
Contact: William S. Robertson, President

The Barker Welfare Foundation
P.O. Box 2
Glen Head, NY 11545
(516) 759-5592
APPLICATION ADDRESS
FOR CHICAGO AGENCIES:
c/o Philip D. Block III
One First National Plaza
Suite 2544
Chicago, IL 60603
TREASURER'S OFFICE:
c/o Charles C. Hickox
26 Broadway
New York, NY 10004

Description: Funding for a wide range of interests, including mental health services and other health services
Restrictions: Giving focused in Chicago, Illinois; Michigan City, Indiana; and New York, New York
$ Given: In FY90, 204 grants totaling $1.7 million were awarded; average range of $3,000 - $9,000 per award
Application Information: Write for application guidelines; see the important information in the chapter introduction about the need for institutional affiliation.
Deadline: Proposals accepted September-December; final applications due February 1
Contact: New York and national agencies: Mrs. Walter L. Ross II, President; Chicago agencies: Philip D. Block III

The Frances L. & Edwin L. Cummings Memorial Fund

For full description see listing under New Jersey

Curtice-Burns/Pro-Fac Foundation
P.O. Box 681
Rochester, NY 14603
(716) 383-1850

Description: Funding for health agencies, including those addressing drug abuse and alcoholism; support for education, human services, community funds, and culture
Restrictions: Giving focused in areas of corporate operations
$ Given: In FY90, grants totaling $436,000 were awarded; average award, $1,000
Application Information: Write for application guidelines; see the important information in the chapter introduction about the need for institutional affiliation.
Deadline: None
Contact: Marilyn T. Helmer, Vice President

Jean and Louis Dreyfus Foundation, Inc.
c/o Decker Hubbard and Welden
30 Rockefeller Plaza
New York, NY 10112
(212) 581-7575

Description: Funding for medical research and arts institutions; additional support for social services, including drug abuse programs
Restrictions: Giving focused in New York City
$ Given: In 1990, 78 grants totaling $724,000 were awarded; average range of $5,000 - $10,000 per award
Application Information: Write for application guidelines; see the important information in the chapter introduction about the need for institutional affiliation.
Deadline: N/A
Contact: Thomas J. Hubbard, Secretary

FLOW-THROUGH FUNDING

. . . .

**The Rosamond Gifford
Charitable Corporation**
731 James Street
Room 404
Syracuse, NY 13203
(315) 474-2489

Description: Funding for urban problems, alcoholism treatment programs, health, education, and other human services
Restrictions: Giving restricted to organizations serving Syracuse and Onandaga County, New York
$ Given: In 1989, 29 grants totaling $756,000 were awarded; average range of $4,000 - $40,000 per award
Application Information: Write for application guidelines; see the important information in the chapter introduction about the need for institutional affiliation.
Deadline: None
Contact: Dean A. Lesinski, Executive Director

**Herman Goldman
Foundation**
61 Broadway
18th Floor
New York, NY 10006
(212) 797-9090

Description: Ongoing support in four funding areas: (1) health, including mental health care services; (2) social justice; (3) education; and (4) the arts
Restrictions: Giving focused in metropolitan New York City
$ Given: In FY90, 128 grants totaling $2 million were awarded; average range of $10,000 - $100,000 per award
Application Information: Write for application guidelines; see the important information in the chapter introduction about the need for institutional affiliation.
Deadlines: Mid-month in January, March, May, July, September, and November
Contact: Richard K. Baron, Executive Director

**Joseph and Sally
Handleman Charitable
Foundation**

For full description see listing under Florida

The IFF Foundation, Inc.
521 West 57th Street
New York, NY 10019
(212) 765-5500

Description: Funding mainly for education and research; some support for hospitals and mental health services
Restrictions: N/A
$ Given: In 1989, 78 grants totaling $376,000 were awarded; range of $100 - $90,000 per award
Application Information: Write for application guidelines; see the important information in the chapter introduction about the need for institutional affiliation.
Deadline: N/A
Contact: John P. Winandy, Treasurer

Ittleson Foundation, Inc.
645 Madison Avenue
16th Floor
New York, NY 10022
(212) 838-5010

Description: Seed money, matching funds, research and special purpose funding to address several areas of interest, including mental health (and the consequences of AIDS on mental health)
Restrictions: No support for direct provision of social services; no support for the humanities
$ Given: In 1990, 99 grants totaling $1.16 million were awarded; range of $50 - $200,000 per award
Application Information: Write for application guidelines; see the important information in the chapter introduction about the need for institutional affiliation.
Deadline: None
Contact: David M. Nee, Executive Director

The J.M. Foundation
60 East 42nd Street
Room 1651
New York, NY 10165
(212) 687-7735

Description: Seed money, research, and special project funding for rehabilitation, including treatment for alcohol and drug abuse; support for several other concerns
Restrictions: No funding for the arts or for international programs
$ Given: In 1990, 86 grants totaling $2.35 million were awarded; average range of $15,000 - $35,000 per award
Application Information: Write for application guidelines; see the important information in the chapter introduction about the need for institutional affiliation.
Deadlines: Proposals accepted in February, July, and October
Contact: Chris K. Olander, Executive Director

**Marion E. Kenworthy -
Sarah H. Swift Foundation,
Inc.**
300 East 34th Street
No. 19C
New York, NY 10016
(212) 685-4918

Description: Funding for social services, mental health services, and other human services
Restrictions: Giving focused mainly in New York, Connecticut, and Washington, DC
$ Given: In 1990, grants totaling $455,000 were awarded; average range of $1,000 - $40,000 per award
Application Information: Write for application guidelines; see the important information in the chapter introduction about the need for institutional affiliation.
Deadlines: April 1 and November 1
Contact: Dr. Maurice V. Russell, Chairman and President

**The Joe and Emily Lowe
Foundation, Inc.**

For full description see listing under Florida

FLOW-THROUGH FUNDING

• •

Metropolitan Life Foundation
One Madison Avenue
New York, NY 10010-3690
(212) 578-6272

Description: Funding for health, including substance abuse programs; support for education, social services, culture, and United Way chapters
Restrictions: No funding for organizations receiving United Way support; no funding for disease-specific organizations; no direct funding to drug treatment centers or community health clinics; several other funding limitations
$ Given: In 1990, 1,000 grants totaling $8.56 million were awarded; average range of $1,000 - $25,000 per award
Application Information: Write for application guidelines; see the important information in the chapter introduction about the need for institutional affiliation.
Deadline: None
Contact: Sibyl C. Jacobson, President and CEO

The Ambrose Monell Foundation
c/o Fulton, Duncombe & Rowe
30 Rockefeller Plaza
Room 3217
New York, NY 10112
(212) 586-0700

Description: General purpose funding for hospitals and health services, medical and chemical research, mental health programs, alcoholism programs, and several other social and cultural concerns
Restrictions: N/A
$ Given: In 1990, 86 grants totaling $6.34 million were awarded; average range of $5,000 - $100,000 per award
Application Information: Write for application guidelines; see the important information in the chapter introduction about the need for institutional affiliation.
Deadline: None
Contact: Harmon Duncombe, President

Mutual of New York Foundation
1740 Broadway
MD 9-5
New York, NY 10019
(212) 708-2136

Description: Special project funding and matching funds for programs that combat social problems, including alcoholism
Restrictions: Giving focused in areas of corporate operations, including Teaneck, New Jersey; Purchase, Syracuse, and New York, New York
$ Given: In 1989, 114 grants totaling $863,000 were awarded; average range of $1,000 - $10,000 per award
Application Information: Write for application guidelines; see the important information in the chapter introduction about the need for institutional affiliation.
Deadline: April 30
Contact: Lynn Stekas, President

The New-Land Foundation, Inc.
1345 Avenue of the Americas
45th Floor
New York, NY 10105
(212) 841-6000

Description: General purpose funding for mental health programs, social service agencies, civil rights, the environment, and culture
Restrictions: N/A
$ Given: In 1990, 111 grants totaling $1.44 million were awarded; average range of $5,000 - $15,000 per award
Application Information: Write for application guidelines; see the important information in the chapter introduction about the need for institutional affiliation.
Deadlines: February 1 and August 1
Contact: Robert Wolf, Esq., President

The New York Community Trust
Two Park Avenue
24th Floor
New York, NY 10016
(212) 686-0010
FAX (212) 532-8528

Description: Seed money and special project funding in several areas of interest: (1) families and youth, including drug abuse issues; (2) community development; (3) education; and (4) health, including mental illness and retardation
Restrictions: Giving focused within the metropolitan New York City area
$ Given: In 1990, 8,253 grants totaling $56.4 million were awarded; average range of $5,000 - $35,000 per award
Application Information: Write for application guidelines; see the important information in the chapter introduction about the need for institutional affiliation.
Deadline: None
Contact: Lorie A. Slutsky, Director

Norwood Foundation, Inc.
c/o Bessemer Trust Co.
630 Fifth Avenue
New York, NY 10111
MAILING ADDRESS:
P.O. Box 238, East Norwich,
NY 11732
(516) 626-0288

Description: Funding for health associations, drug abuse programs, education, hospitals, and culture
Restrictions: Giving focused mainly in New York
$ Given: In 1990, 16 grants totaling $97,000 were awarded; average range of $1,000 - $25,000 per award
Application Information: Write for application guidelines; see the important information in the chapter introduction about the need for institutional affiliation.
Deadline: None
Contact: Thomas M. Bancroft, Jr., President and Treasurer

FLOW-THROUGH FUNDING

• • • • • • • • • • • • • • • • • •

Moses L. Parshelsky Foundation
26 Court Street
Room 904
Brooklyn, NY 11242
(718) 875-8883

Description: Special project funding for hospitals, mental health programs, education, religious activities, and Jewish welfare
Restrictions: Giving focused in Brooklyn and Queens, New York
$ Given: In 1990, 60 grants totaling $288,300 were awarded; average range of $100 - $30,000 per award
Application Information: Write for application guidelines; see the important information in the chapter introduction about the need for institutional affiliation.
Deadline: May 31
Contact: Tony B. Berk, Trustee

Joseph H. and Florence A. Roblee Foundation

For full description see listing under Missouri

Saltzman Foundation, Inc.
350 Fifth Avenue
New York, NY 10118-0001

Description: Funding for mental health, hospitals, education, culture, and international affairs
Restrictions: Giving focused in New York
$ Given: In FY90, 27 grants totaling $54,400 were awarded; range of $50 - $11,500 per award
Application Information: Write for application guidelines; see the important information in the chapter introduction about the need for institutional affiliation.
Deadline: None
Contact: Arnold A. Saltzman, President

The Christopher D. Smithers Foundation, Inc.
P.O. Box 67
Oyster Bay Road
Mill Neck, NY 11765
(516) 676-0067

Description: Funding for alcoholism prevention, treatment, and research; creates educational booklets on alcoholism
Restrictions: N/A
$ Given: In 1990, 38 grants totaling $339,000 were awarded; range of $100 - $75,000 per award
Application Information: Write for application guidelines; see the important information in the chapter introduction about the need for institutional affiliation.
Deadline: Proposals accepted September through December
Contact: Adele C. Smithers, President

• • • • • • • • • • • • • • • • • • • •

Nate B. and Frances Spingold Foundation, Inc.
c/o Lankenau & Bickford
1740 Broadway
New York, NY 10019
(212) 489-8230

Description: General purpose funding for mental health, public education, and Jewish affairs
Restrictions: Giving focused in metropolitan New York City
$ Given: In FY90, 8 grants totaling $233,000 were awarded; average range of $10,000 - $50,000 per award
Application Information: Write for application guidelines; see the important information in the chapter introduction about the need for institutional affiliation.
Deadline: None
Contact: Daniel L. Kurtz, President

Irvin Stern Foundation

For full description see listing under Illinois

Stepping Stones Foundation
P.O. Box 452
Bedford Hills, NY 10507

Description: Funding for organizations offering help to alcoholics, as well as to their families, friends, and associates
Restrictions: N/A
$ Given: In 1989, grants totaling $313,000 were awarded
Application Information: Write for application guidelines; see the important information in the chapter introduction about the need for institutional affiliation.
Deadline: N/A
Contact: Eileen Lang, Administrator

van Ameringen Foundation, Inc.
509 Madison Avenue
New York, NY 10022
(212) 758-6221

Description: Funding to promote mental health and social welfare; support for psychology and psychiatry; funding for child development and medical education
Restrictions: Giving focused in the urban Northeast, including Boston, Philadelphia, Baltimore, New York, and Washington, DC; no support for mental retardation or substance abuse
$ Given: In 1990, 56 grants totaling $1.7 million were awarded; average range of $20,000 - $50,000 per award
Application Information: Write for application guidelines; see the important information in the chapter introduction about the need for institutional affiliation.
Deadlines: January, April, and September
Contact: Patricia Kind, President

FLOW-THROUGH FUNDING

• • • • • • • • • • • • • • • • •

NORTH CAROLINA

Pearl Dixon Balthis Foundation
c/o First Union National Bank
Capital Management Group
CMG-10-1159
Charlotte, NC 28288-1159
(704) 374-6593

Description: General purpose funding for mental health, social services, youth agencies, education, religious organizations, and other human services
Restrictions: Giving strictly limited to North Carolina, with emphasis on the Western Piedmont area
$ Given: In FY90, 19 grants totaling $76,000 were awarded; range of $500 - $10,000 per award
Application Information: Write for application guidelines; see the important information in the chapter introduction about the need for institutional affiliation.
Deadlines: May 1 and December 1
Contact: Kenneth R. Brown

Camp Foundation

For full description see listing under Virginia

Harry L. Dalton Foundation, Inc.
736 Wachovia Center
Charlotte, NC 28285
(704) 332-5380

Description: Funding for mental health, drug abuse, education, cultural programs, family planning, and historic preservation
Restrictions: N/A
$ Given: In FY89, 31 grants totaling $80,200 were awarded; range of $20 - $21,300 per award
Application Information: Write for application guidelines; see the important information in the chapter introduction about the need for institutional affiliation.
Deadline: None
Contact: Harry L. Dalton, President

Carrie C. & Lena V. Glenn Foundation
c/o Branch Banking & Trust Co.
223 West Nash Street
Wilson, NC 27893

Description: Funding for health, drug abuse, education, culture, and other concerns
Restrictions: Giving focused in Gaston County, North Carolina
$ Given: In FY90, 18 grants totaling $185,000 were awarded; range of $1,000 - $50,000 per award
Application Information: Write for application guidelines; see the important information in the chapter introduction about the need for institutional affiliation.
Deadline: None

• • • • • • • • • • • • • • • • • • • •

Integon Foundation
500 West Fifth Street
Winston-Salem, NC 27152
(919) 770-2000

Description: Special project funding for human services, including drug abuse programs; support for community development, culture, and the United Way
Restrictions: Giving focused in Winston-Salem, North Carolina, with some funding in the Piedmont area
$ Given: In 1989, 36 grants totaling $156,000 were awarded; range of $100 - $42,000 per award
Application Information: Write for application guidelines; see the important information in the chapter introduction about the need for institutional affiliation.
Deadlines: January, April, July, and October
Contact: Turner Coley

Minnesota Mining and Manu-facturing Foundation, Inc.

For full description see listing under Minnesota

**Kate B. Reynolds
Charitable Trust**
2422 Reynolda Road
Winston-Salem, NC 27106
(919) 723-1456

Description: Funding for rural health services, including alcoholism and drug abuse programs; 75% of monies are distributed statewide; 25% are distributed for needy residents in Winston-Salem and Forsyth County, North Carolina
Restrictions: Giving strictly limited to North Carolina
$ Given: In FY90, 97 grants totaling $7.44 million were awarded; average range of $10,000 - $100,000 per award
Application Information: Write for application guidelines; see the important information in the chapter introduction about the need for institutional affiliation.
Deadlines: April 1 and October 1
Contact: Edwin W. Monroe, M.D., Executive Director; E. Ray Cope, Deputy Executive Director; or W. Vance Frye, Associate Director

Joseph H. and Florence A. Roblee Foundation

For full description see listing under Missouri

143

FLOW-THROUGH FUNDING

. . . .

NORTH DAKOTA

Minnesota Mining and Manu-
facturing Foundation, Inc.

For full description see listing under Minnesota

North Dakota Community
Foundation
P.O. Box 387
Bismarck, ND 58502-0387
(701) 222-8349

Description: Funding to aid the elderly/disadvantaged;
support for health services, including mental health services
Restrictions: Giving focused in North Dakota
$ Given: In 1990, 178 grants totaling $230,000 were
awarded; range of $60 - $10,000 per award
Application Information: Application by foundation
invitation only
Deadline: August 31
Contact: Richard H. Timmins, President

Alex Stern Family
Foundation
Bill Stern Building
Suite 202
609-1/2 First Avenue, North
Fargo, ND 58102
(701) 237-0170

Description: Funding for culture, social services (incl.
alcohol abuse programs), education, health, and community
organizations
Restrictions: Giving focused in Fargo, North Dakota and
Moorhead, Minnesota
$ Given: In 1989, 49 grants totaling $343,000 were awarded;
range of $1,000 - $30,000 per award
Application Information: Write for application guidelines;
see the important information in the chapter introduction
about the need for institutional affiliation.
Deadline: Proposals accepted April through December
Contact: A.M. Eriksmoen, Executive Director

OHIO

The Andrews Foundation
1127 Euclid Avenue
Suite 210
Cleveland, OH 44115
(216) 621-3215

Description: General purpose funding for alcoholism,
education, the handicapped, and performing arts
Restrictions: Giving focused in northeastern Ohio
$ Given: In 1990, 27 grants totaling $210,000 were awarded;
average range of $1,000 - $25,000 per award
Application Information: Write for application guidelines;
see the important information in the chapter introduction
about the need for institutional affiliation.
Deadline: None
Contact: Richard S. Tomer, President

• •

The Columbus Foundation
1234 East Broad Street
Columbus, OH 43205
(614) 251-4000

Description: Funding for distribution to local charitable organizations; support in the following areas: health, mental health, mental retardation, the humanities, education, civic affairs, the environment, and social services
Restrictions: Giving focused in central Ohio
$ Given: In 1990, 1,906 grants totaling $11.44 million were awarded; average range of $1,000 - $50,000 per award
Application Information: Write for application guidelines; see the important information in the chapter introduction about the need for institutional affiliation.
Deadline: Varies
Contact: James I. Luck, President

James M. Cox, Jr. Foundation, Inc.
Fourth and Ludlow Streets
Dayton, OH 45402
APPLICATION ADDRESS:
c/o Cox Enterprises, Inc.
P.O. Box 105720
Atlanta, GA 30348

Description: General purpose funding for mental health, education, culture, and the environment
Restrictions: Giving focused in Ohio and Georgia
$ Given: In 1989, 5 grants totaling $305,000 were awarded; range of $5,000 - $200,000 per award
Application Information: Write for application guidelines; see the important information in the chapter introduction about the need for institutional affiliation.
Deadline: None
Contact: Carl R. Gross, Treasurer

Forest City Enterprises Charitable Foundation, Inc.
10800 Brookpark Road
Cleveland, OH 44130

Description: Funding for drug abuse programs, as well as for Jewish welfare funds, a community fund, education, culture, and human services
Restrictions: Giving focused in Ohio
$ Given: In FY90, 300 grants totaling $678,000 were awarded; range of $25 - $100,000 per award
Application Information: Write for application guidelines; see the important information in the chapter introduction about the need for institutional affiliation.
Deadline: None
Contact: Nathan Shafran

FLOW-THROUGH FUNDING

• • • • • • • • • • • • • • • • • • • •

The Hamilton Community Foundation, Inc.
319 North Third Street
Hamilton, OH 45011
(513) 863-1389

Description: Seed money and special project funding for health agencies, including drug and alcohol abuse rehabilitation programs; support for youth welfare agencies and cultural programs
Restrictions: Giving only for Butler County, Ohio; no general purpose support
$ Given: In 1990, 250 grants totaling $1.2 million were awarded; range of $20 - $108,000 per award
Application Information: Write for application guidelines; see the important information in the chapter introduction about the need for institutional affiliation.
Deadline: Varies
Contact: Cynthia V. Parrish, Executive Director

Hexcel Foundation

For full description see listing under California

The Huffy Foundation, Inc.
P.O. Box 1204
Dayton, OH 45401
(513) 866-6251

Description: Funding for human services, programs for drug/ alcohol abusers, health and hospitals, education, and civic affairs
Restrictions: Giving focused in areas of corporate operations in California, Colorado, Ohio, Pennsylvania, and Wisconsin
$ Given: In FY91, 97 grants totaling $274,500 were awarded; range of $1,000 - $20,000 per award
Application Information: Write for application guidelines; see the important information in the chapter introduction about the need for institutional affiliation.
Deadline: None
Contact: Robert R. Wieland, Secretary

Iddings Foundation
Kettering Tower
Suite 1620
Dayton, OH 45423
(513) 224-1773

Description: Funding for health care, mental health, education, culture, and other concerns
Restrictions: Giving only in Ohio, with focus on metropolitan Dayton
$ Given: In 1989, 79 grants totaling $489,000 were awarded; average range of $5 - $10,000 per award
Application Information: Write for application guidelines; see the important information in the chapter introduction about the need for institutional affiliation.
Deadlines: March 1, June 1, September 1, and November 1
Contact: Maribeth A. Eiken, Administrative Secretary

• • • • • • • • • • • • • • • • • • • •

William H. Kilcawley Fund
c/o The Dollar Savings &
Trust Co.
P.O. Box 450
Youngstown, OH 44501-0450
(216) 744-9000

Description: General purpose funding for alcohol abuse programs, as well as for education, Christian churches, the arts, health and social services, and community funds
Restrictions: Giving focused in Ohio
$ Given: In 1990, 22 grants totaling $124,000 were awarded; average range of $500 - $25,000 per award
Application Information: Write for application guidelines; see the important information in the chapter introduction about the need for institutional affiliation.
Deadline: None
Contact: Herbert H. Pridham

The Kroger Company Foundation
1014 Vine Street
Cincinnati, OH 45201
(513) 762-4443
APPLICATION ADDRESS:
P.O. Box 1199, Cincinnati,
OH 45201-1199

Description: General purpose funding for human service and substance abuse programs, as well as for education, culture, and civic affairs in corporate areas
Restrictions: Giving focused in areas of corporate operations
$ Given: In 1990, 1,400 grants totaling $4 million were awarded; average range of $1,000 - $20,000 per award
Application Information: Write for application guidelines; see the important information in the chapter introduction about the need for institutional affiliation.
Deadline: None
Contact: Paul Bernish, Vice President

The S. Livingston Mather Charitable Trust
803 Tower East
20600 Chagrin Boulevard
Shaker Heights, OH 44122
(216) 942-6484

Description: Funding for social services, mental health, education, welfare, the environment, and culture
Restrictions: Giving focused in northeastern Ohio
$ Given: In 1990, 49 grants totaling $143,600 were awarded; average range of $1,000 - $10,000 per award
Application Information: Write for application guidelines; see the important information in the chapter introduction about the need for institutional affiliation.
Deadline: None
Contact: S. Sterling McMillan, Secretary

**Minnesota Mining and Manu-
facturing Foundation, Inc.**

For full description see listing under Minnesota

FLOW-THROUGH FUNDING

•   •   •   •   •   •   •   •   •   •   •   •   •   •   •   •   •   •   •   •

Burton D. Morgan Foundation, Inc.
P.O. Box 1500
Akron, OH 44309-1500
(216) 258-6512

Description: General purpose funding for mental health, education, religion, and culture
Restrictions: Giving focused in Summit County, Ohio
$ Given: In 1990, 41 grants totaling $434,000 were awarded; range of $500 - $100,000 per award
Application Information: Write for application guidelines; see the important information in the chapter introduction about the need for institutional affiliation.
Deadline: None
Contact: John V. Frank, President

The Nordson Corporation Foundation
28601 Clemens Road
Westlake, OH 44145-1148
(216) 892-1580
(216) 988-9411

Description: Funding for community programs in education, human welfare, culture, and civic affairs; support for mental health and alcoholism programs, among other things
Restrictions: Giving focused in northern Ohio and Atlanta, Georgia
$ Given: In FY90, 51 grants totaling $311,000 were awarded; average range of $500 - $25,000 per award
Application Information: Write for application guidelines; see the important information in the chapter introduction about the need for institutional affiliation.
Deadline: None
Contact: James C. Doughman, Director, Public Affairs

The Van Wert County Foundation
101-1/2 East Main Street
Van Wert, OH 45891
(419) 238-1743

Description: General purpose funding for alcoholism and drug abuse programs, as well as for education, youth agencies, and art/recreation facilities
Restrictions: Giving only in Van Wert County, Ohio
$ Given: In 1990, 18 grants totaling $210,000 were awarded; range of $50 - $60,000 per award
Application Information: Write for application guidelines; see the important information in the chapter introduction about the need for institutional affiliation.
Deadlines: May 15 and November 15
Contact: Robert W. Games, Executive Secretary

Women's Project Foundation
c/o Ameritrust Co., N.A.
P.O. Box 5937
Cleveland, OH 44101-0937
(216) 737-5283

Description: Research and special project funding for women's/children's issues; support for alcoholism programs
Restrictions: N/A
$ Given: In FY90, 4 grants totaling $332,000 were awarded; range of $10,000 - $160,000 per award
Application Information: Write for application guidelines; see the important information in the chapter introduction about the need for institutional affiliation.
Deadline: November 1
Contact: Joyce K. Alexander

OKLAHOMA

Minnesota Mining and Manufacturing Foundation, Inc.

For full description see listing under Minnesota

Red River Valley Council for the Aid of Persons with Mental Problems, Inc.

For full description see listing under Texas

The Anne and Henry Zarrow Foundation
P.O. Box 1530
Tulsa, OK 74101
(918) 587-3391

Description: Funding for health, mental health, medical research, education, the handicapped, and disadvantaged populations
Restrictions: Giving focused in Tulsa, Oklahoma
$ Given: In 1989, 48 grants totaling $289,000 were awarded; range of $1,000 - $30,000 per award
Application Information: Write for application guidelines; see the important information in the chapter introduction about the need for institutional affiliation.
Deadline: None
Contact: Judith Z. Kishner

FLOW-THROUGH FUNDING

• •

OREGON

The Carpenter Foundation
711 East Main Street
Suite 18
P.O. Box 816
Medford, OR 97501
(503) 772-5851

Description: Funding for social services, drug abuse programs, education, welfare, and other concerns
Restrictions: Giving focused in Jackson and Josephine counties, Oregon
$ Given: In FY91, grants totaling $451,500 were awarded
Application Information: Write for application guidelines; see the important information in the chapter introduction about the need for institutional affiliation.
Deadlines: Quarterly
Contact: Dunbar Carpenter, Treasurer

Heileman Old Style Foundation, Inc.

For full description see listing under Wisconsin

The Samuel S. Johnson Foundation
P.O. Box 356
Redmond, OR 97756
(503) 548-8104

Description: Funding in several areas of interest, including drug abuse prevention, social services, education, health and hospitals, civic affairs, and culture
Restrictions: Giving focused in Oregon, northern California, and Washington
$ Given: In FY90, 106 grants totaling $182,000 were awarded; average range of $500 - $1,000 per award
Application Information: Write for application guidelines; see the important information in the chapter introduction about the need for institutional affiliation.
Deadlines: June 1 and November 15
Contact: Elizabeth Hill Johnson, President

Minnesota Mining and Manufacturing Foundation, Inc.

For full description see listing under Minnesota

Ray Foundation

For full description see listing under Washington

PENNSYLVANIA

Isaac and Carol Auerbach Family Foundation
900 Centennial Road
Narberth, PA 19072-1408
(215) 667-8090

Description: Funding for mental health, health associations, education, culture, and Jewish giving
Restrictions: N/A
$ Given: In FY90, 96 grants totaling $39,000 were awarded; range of $10 - $15,000 per award
Application Information: Write for application guidelines; see the important information in the chapter introduction about the need for institutional affiliation.
Deadline: None
Contact: Isaac L. Auerbach, Trustee

The Downs Foundation
P.O. Box 475
Davisville Road and Turnpike Drive
Willow Grove, PA 19090
(215) 672-1100

Description: General purpose funding for health and social services, including a drug and alcohol program; support for employee scholarship program (Downs Carpet Co.)
Restrictions: Giving focused in Philadelphia, Pennsylvania
$ Given: In 1990, 49 grants totaling $66,000 were awarded; range of $100 - $10,000 per award
Application Information: Write for application guidelines; see the important information in the chapter introduction about the need for institutional affiliation.
Deadline: None
Contact: T. George Downs, Trustee

Heileman Old Style Foundation, Inc.

For full description see listing under Wisconsin

Maurice Falk Medical Fund
3315 Grant Building
Pittsburgh, PA 15219
(412) 261-2485

Description: Funding for mental health programs, as well as for public policy and minority affairs
Restrictions: N/A
$ Given: In FY90, 60 grants totaling $163,000 were awarded; range of $250 - $21,000 per award
Application Information: Write for application guidelines; see the important information in the chapter introduction about the need for institutional affiliation.
Deadline: None
Contact: Philip B. Hallen, President

FLOW-THROUGH FUNDING

. . . .

Hexcel Foundation   **For full description see listing under California**

The Huffy Foundation, Inc.   **For full description see listing under Ohio**

Edith C. Justus Trust
National Transit Building
Oil City, PA 16301
(814) 677-5085

Description: General purpose funding for social service and health agencies, including those with alcoholism programs; support for community development
Restrictions: Giving focused in Venango County, Pennsylvania, with emphasis on Oil City
$ Given: In 1990, 22 grants totaling $230,000 were awarded; average range of $5,000 - $20,000 per award
Application Information: Write for application guidelines; see the important information in the chapter introduction about the need for institutional affiliation.
Deadline: Proposals accepted in April, August, and November
Contact: Stephen P. Kosak, Consultant

Minnesota Mining and Manu-   **For full description see listing under Minnesota**
facturing Foundation, Inc.

G.C. Murphy Company Foundation
211 Oberdick Drive
McKeesport, PA 15135
(412) 751-6649

Description: Funding for health associations and services, including programs for the mentally ill; support for youth and social services
Restrictions: Giving focused in southwestern Allegheny County, Pennsylvania
$ Given: In 1990, 26 grants totaling $139,000 were awarded; range of $1,000 - $15,000 per award
Application Information: Write for application guidelines; see the important information in the chapter introduction about the need for institutional affiliation.
Deadline: None
Contact: Edwin W. Davis, Secretary

The Pew Charitable Trusts
Three Parkway
Suite 501
Philadelphia, PA 19102

Description: Funding for health care delivery systems, especially for the physically and/or mentally handicapped; support for culture, education, the environment, and human services
Restrictions: N/A
$ Given: Grants totaling $137.1 million were awarded
Application Information: Write for application guidelines; see the important information in the chapter introduction about the need for institutional affiliation.
Deadline: None
Contact: Rebecca W. Rimel, Executive Director

The Rockwell Foundation
3212 USX Tower
600 Grant Street
Pittsburgh, PA 15219
(412) 765-3990

Description: Funding for hospitals and health agencies, including programs for mental illness and drug abuse; support for education, culture, family services, and other concerns
Restrictions: Giving focused in Pennsylvania
$ Given: In 1990, 100 grants totaling $440,000 were awarded; range of $100 - $75,000 per award
Application Information: Write for application guidelines; see the important information in the chapter introduction about the need for institutional affiliation.
Deadline: Varies
Contact: H. Campbell Stuckeman, Secretary

Scaife Family Foundation
Three Mellon Bank Center
525 William Penn Place
Suite 3900
Pittsburgh, PA 15219-1708
(412) 392-2900

Description: General purpose funding for programs addressing family issues, including drug abuse and alcoholism programs
Restrictions: N/A
$ Given: In 1990, 73 grants totaling $4.7 million were awarded; average range of $25,000 - $50,000 per award
Application Information: Write for application guidelines; see the important information in the chapter introduction about the need for institutional affiliation.
Deadline: None
Contact: Joanne B. Beyer, Vice President

. . . .

Stackpole-Hall Foundation
44 South St. Marys Street
St. Marys, PA 15857
(814) 834-1845

Description: Funding for health services, including mental health and drug abuse programs; support for education, social services, community development, and the arts
Restrictions: Giving focused in Elk County, Pennsylvania
$ Given: In 1990, 63 grants totaling $606,000 were awarded; range of $200 - $70,000 per award
Application Information: Write for application guidelines; see the important information in the chapter introduction about the need for institutional affiliation.
Deadline: None
Contact: William C. Conrad, Executive Secretary

Staunton Farm Foundation
Centre City Tower
Suite 240
650 Smithfield Street
Pittsburgh, PA 15222
(412) 281-8020
APPLICATION ADDRESS:
3317 Grant Building
Pittsburgh, PA 15219
(412) 261-2485

Description: Funding for local organizations dealing with mental health, the emotionally handicapped, and child welfare
Restrictions: Giving focused in Allegheny County, Pennsylvania and contiguous counties
$ Given: In 1990, 25 grants totaling $747,000 were awarded; average range of $10,000 - $50,000 per award
Application Information: Write for application guidelines; see the important information in the chapter introduction about the need for institutional affiliation.
Deadlines: Mid-month in January, April, July, and October
Contact: Marilyn Ingalls, Grants Administrator

USX Foundation, Inc.

For full description see listing under Minnesota

van Ameringen Foundation, Inc.

For full description see listing under New York

PUERTO RICO

Puerto Rico Community Foundation
Royal Bank Center Building
Suite 1417
Hato Rey, PR 00917
(809) 751-3822
(809) 751-3885

Description: Funding for improvement of Puerto Rico's economy and standard of living; support for drug and alcohol abuse programs, as well as for many other efforts
Restrictions: Giving strictly limited to Puerto Rico
$ Given: In 1990, 42 grants totaling $1.3 million were awarded; range of $2,500 - $136,000 per award
Application Information: Write for application guidelines; see the important information in the chapter introduction about the need for institutional affiliation.
Deadline: None
Contact: Jose R. Crespo, Administrator

RHODE ISLAND

Joseph W. Martin Trust
781 Main Street
Warren, RI 02885-4320
(401) 331-8842

Description: Funding for medical assistance for women, including mental health services, health services, and nursing
Restrictions: Giving in Warren, Rhode Island only
$ Given: In FY90, 4 grants totaling $44,000 were awarded; range of $5,000 - $18,000 per award
Application Information: Write for application guidelines; see the important information in the chapter introduction about the need for institutional affiliation.
Deadline: N/A
Contact: S. George McVey, Trustee

SOUTH CAROLINA

Minnesota Mining and Manufacturing Foundation, Inc.
3M Center
Building 521-11-01
St. Paul, MN 55144-1000
(612) 736-3781

Description: Funding for human services, including programs for alcohol and drug abuse; support for education, the arts, preventive health care, and community funds
Restrictions: Giving focused in areas with corporate facilities, including areas in South Carolina
$ Given: In 1989, grants totaling $8.5 million were awarded; average range of $500 - $25,000 per award
Application Information: Write for application guidelines; see the important information in the chapter introduction about the need for institutional affiliation.
Deadlines: 8 weeks prior to board meetings; board meets in March, August, and December
Contact: Eugene W. Steele, Secretary

• • • • • • • • • • • • • • • • • • • •

SOUTH DAKOTA

Minnesota Mining and Manufacturing Foundation, Inc.
3M Center
Building 521-11-01
St. Paul, MN 55144-1000
(612) 736-3781

Description: Funding for human services, including programs for alcohol and drug abuse; support for education, the arts, preventive health care, and community funds
Restrictions: Giving focused in areas with corporate facilities, including areas in Alabama, California, Georgia, Illinois, Indiana, Iowa, Kentucky, Massachusetts, Michigan, Minnesota, Mississippi, Missouri, Nebraska, New Jersey, North Carolina, North Dakota, Ohio, Oklahoma, Oregon, Pennsylvania, South Carolina, South Dakota, Texas, Utah, Virginia, Washington, West Virginia, and Wisconsin
$ Given: In 1989, grants totaling $8.5 million were awarded; average range of $500 - $25,000 per award
Application Information: Write for application guidelines; see the important information in the chapter introduction about the need for institutional affiliation.
Deadlines: 8 weeks prior to board meetings; board meets in March, August, and December
Contact: Eugene W. Steele, Secretary

TENNESSEE

Aladdin Industries Foundation, Inc.
703 Murfreesboro Road
Nashville, TN 37210-4521
(615) 748-3360

Description: General purpose funding for drug abuse programs, education, music, business, the elderly, and youth
Restrictions: Giving focused in Tennessee
$ Given: In 1990, 19 grants totaling $65,500 were awarded; range of $500 - $20,000 per award
Application Information: Write for application guidelines; see the important information in the chapter introduction about the need for institutional affiliation.
Deadline: Varies
Contact: L.B. Jenkins, Secretary-Treasurer

Dantzler Bond Ansley Foundation
c/o Third National Bank
Trust Department
P.O. Box 305110
Nashville, TN 37230-5110
(615) 748-5207

Description: Funding for health, alcoholism programs, medical research, education, social services, and culture
Restrictions: Giving focused in central Tennessee, especially Nashville
$ Given: In FY89, 42 grants totaling $244,500 were awarded; range of $500 - $50,000 per award
Application Information: Write for application guidelines; see the important information in the chapter introduction about the need for institutional affiliation.
Deadline: May 31
Contact: Kim Williams, Trust Officer, Third National Bank

Joe C. Davis Foundation
28 White Bridge Road
Nashville, TN 37205
APPLICATION ADDRESS:
908 Audubon Road
Nashville, TN 37204
(615) 297-1030

Description: Funding for health, alcoholism and drug abuse programs, medical research, and education
Restrictions: Giving focused in Nashville, Tennessee
$ Given: In FY90, 67 grants totaling $292,000 were awarded; range of $200 - $50,000 per award
Application Information: Write for application guidelines; see the important information in the chapter introduction about the need for institutional affiliation.
Deadline: August 15
Contact: Mrs. Anne Fergerson

H.W. Durham Foundation
5050 Poplar Avenue
Suite 1522
Memphis, TN 38157
(901) 683-3583

Description: Seed money, research and special project funding for projects addressing problems of the aging process; support for mental health issues
Restrictions: Giving focused in Memphis, Tennessee
$ Given: In FY90, 19 grants totaling $403,600 were awarded; average range of $1,500 - $64,000 per award
Application Information: Write for application guidelines; see the important information in the chapter introduction about the need for institutional affiliation.
Deadlines: January 1, April 1, and August 1
Contact: Jenks McCrory, Program Director

FLOW-THROUGH FUNDING

• • • • • • • • • • • • • • • • • • • •

Virginia and George Scholze, Jr. Foundation
MacLellan Building
3rd Floor
Chattanooga, TN 37402

Description: Funding for programs and organizations seeking to eliminate alcoholism and other drug addictions in Tennessee
Restrictions: Giving focused in Chattanooga, Tennessee
$ Given: 3 grants totaling $180,000 were awarded; range of $20,000 - $130,000 per award
Application Information: Write for application guidelines; see the important information in the chapter introduction about the need for institutional affiliation.
Deadline: None
Contact: John C. Stophel, President

TEXAS

Coastal Bend Community Foundation
860 First City Bank Tower
FCB 276
Corpus Christi, TX 78477
(512) 882-9745

Description: Funding for social services, including alcohol and drug abuse programs; support for welfare, hospitals, education, community development, and culture
Restrictions: Giving strictly limited to the following Texas counties: Aransas, Bee, Jim Wells, Kleberg, Nueces, Refugio, and San Patricio
$ Given: In 1989, 171 grants totaling $521,500 were awarded; average range of $1,000 - $5,000 per award
Application Information: Write for application guidelines; see the important information in the chapter introduction about the need for institutional affiliation.
Deadline: September 15
Contact: Dana Williams, Executive Vice President

The Constantin Foundation
3811 Turtle Creek Boulevard
Suite 320-LB 39
Dallas, TX 75219
(214) 522-9300

Description: Funding for health and social service programs, including drug and alcohol abuse programs; support for education, culture, hospitals, and youth agencies
Restrictions: Giving focused in metropolitan Dallas, Texas
$ Given: In 1989, 32 grants totaling $1.17 million were awarded; range of $2,000 - $200,000 per award
Application Information: Write for application guidelines; see the important information in the chapter introduction about the need for institutional affiliation.
Deadline: September 30
Contact: Betty S. Hillin, Executive Director

. . . .

The Cullen Foundation
601 Jefferson
40th Floor
Houston, TX 77002
(713) 651-8600
MAILING ADDRESS:
P.O. Box 1600
Houston, TX 77251

Description: Funding for social services, drug abuse prevention, and several other medical, educational, and charitable concerns
Restrictions: Giving strictly limited to Texas, with focus on Houston
$ Given: In 1990, 36 grants totaling $11 million were awarded; average range of $30,000 - $110,000 per award
Application Information: Write for application guidelines; see the important information in the chapter introduction about the need for institutional affiliation.
Deadline: None
Contact: Joseph C. Graf, Executive Secretary

Theodore P. Davis Charitable Trust
c/o Texas Commerce Bank
Trust Department
700 Lavaca
Austin, TX 78701

Description: Funding for alcoholism and drug abuse programs, social services, women's services, the homeless, and vocational education
Restrictions: Giving focused in Austin, Texas
$ Given: In 1990, 11 grants totaling $63,000 were awarded; range of $3,000 - $8,000 per award
Application Information: Write for application guidelines; see the important information in the chapter introduction about the need for institutional affiliation.
Deadline: N/A
Contact: Billy Ramsey, Trustee

Exxon Company
P.O. Box 2180
Houston, TX 77252
(713) 656-9199

Description: Funding for health awards to community clinics, hospices, drug abuse and mental health programs, and programs for the mentally handicapped; support also for community affairs and the arts
Restrictions: Giving focused in areas of corporate operations
$ Given: Grant range of $1,000 - $20,000 per award
Application Information: Write for application guidelines; see the important information in the chapter introduction about the need for institutional affiliation.
Deadline: None
Contact: A.G. Randol III, Operations Coordinator

FLOW-THROUGH FUNDING

• • • • • • • • • • • • • • • • • • •

The Fasken Foundation
500 West Texas Avenue
Suite 1160
Midland, TX 79701
(915) 683-5401

Description: Funding for health and social services, including programs for mental illness, alcoholism, drug abuse, and rehabilitation; support for education (scholarships)
Restrictions: Giving focused in Midland, Texas
$ Given: In 1989, 52 grants totaling $700,000 were awarded; average range of $1,500 - $25,000 per award
Application Information: Write for application guidelines; see the important information in the chapter introduction about the need for institutional affiliation.
Deadlines: Proposals accepted in July and December
Contact: B.L. Jones, Executive Director

Leland Fikes Foundation, Inc.
3050 Lincoln Plaza
500 North Akard
Dallas, TX 75201
(214) 754-0144

Description: Funding for mental health, health and social services, drug abuse programs, medical research, education, and culture
Restrictions: Giving focused in Dallas, Texas
$ Given: In 1989, 122 grants totaling $5.3 million were awarded; range of $500 - $2 million per award
Application Information: Write for application guidelines; see the important information in the chapter introduction about the need for institutional affiliation.
Deadline: None
Contact: Nancy Solana, Research and Grant Administration

The Frees Foundation
5373 West Alabama
Suite 404
Houston, TX 77056
(713) 623-0515

Description: Funding for community organizations, including those providing mental health services and drug abuse programs; support for health associations, hospitals, family services, and international relief organizations
Restrictions: Giving focused in Texas and Mexico
$ Given: In 1989, 13 grants totaling $153,600 were awarded; average range of $1,000 - $100,000 per award
Application Information: Write for application guidelines; see the important information in the chapter introduction about the need for institutional affiliation.
Deadline: None
Contact: Nancy Frees Rosser, Director

Gray Foundation
P.O. Box 45
Houston, TX 77001

Description: Funding for health services, alcoholism programs, education, religion, and other concerns
Restrictions: Giving focused in the southwestern United States
$ Given: In FY90, 63 grants totaling $63,500 were awarded; range of $500 - $6,000 per award
Application Information: Write for application guidelines; see the important information in the chapter introduction about the need for institutional affiliation.
Deadline: June 30
Contact: Emily Gray Elmore, President; or Elaine Gray, VP

Gulf Coast Medical Foundation
P.O. Box 30
Wharton, TX 77488
(409) 532-0904

Description: Funding for medical-related projects, including mental health programs
Restrictions: Giving focused in the following Texas counties: Wharton, Matagorda, Jackson, Colorado, Fort Bend, and Brazoria
$ Given: In FY89, 13 grants totaling $429,400 were awarded; range of $100 - $115,000 per award
Application Information: Write for application guidelines; see the important information in the chapter introduction about the need for institutional affiliation.
Deadline: None
Contact: Dee McElroy, Executive Vice President

Paul and Mary Haas Foundation
P.O. Box 2928
Corpus Christi, TX 78403
(512) 887-6955

Description: Funding for social services and youth agencies, including alcohol abuse programs; support for education, medical research, and culture
Restrictions: Giving focused in Corpus Christi, Texas
$ Given: In 1990, 100 grants totaling $532,000 were awarded; range of $50 - $132,500 per award
Application Information: Write for application guidelines; see the important information in the chapter introduction about the need for institutional affiliation.
Deadline: None
Contact: Nancy Wise Somers, Executive Director

FLOW-THROUGH FUNDING

• • • • • • • • • • • • • • • • • •

G.A.C. Halff Foundation
745 East Mulberry
Suite 400
San Antonio, TX 78212
(512) 735-3300

Description: Funding for social services, drug abuse programs, and other concerns
Restrictions: Giving focused in San Antonio, Texas
$ Given: In FY89, 28 grants totaling $235,000 were awarded; range of $2,000 - $55,000 per award
Application Information: Write for application guidelines; see the important information in the chapter introduction about the need for institutional affiliation.
Deadline: May 15
Contact: Thomas F. Bibb, Vice President

Heileman Old Style Foundation, Inc.

For full description see listing under Wisconsin

Simon and Louise Henderson Foundation
P.O. Box 1365
Lufkin, TX 75902
(409) 634-3448

Description: Funding for drug abuse and alcoholism programs, hospitals, education, and Protestant giving
Restrictions: Giving focused in eastern Texas
$ Given: In 1989, 21 grants totaling $146,600 were awarded; range of $1,000 - $20,000 per award
Application Information: Write for application guidelines; see the important information in the chapter introduction about the need for institutional affiliation.
Deadline: None
Contact: Simon W. Henderson, Jr., President

Hexcel Foundation

For full description see listing under California

Hillcrest Foundation
c/o NCNB Texas National Bank
Trust Division
P.O. Box 830241
Dallas, TX 75283-0241
(214) 508-1965

Description: Funding for health and social services, including drug abuse programs; support for education, housing, hospitals, and other concerns
Restrictions: Giving strictly limited to Texas, with focus on Dallas
$ Given: In FY90, 128 grants totaling $3.2 million were awarded; average range of $1,000 - $250,000 per award
Application Information: Write for application guidelines; see the important information in the chapter introduction about the need for institutional affiliation.
Deadline: None
Contact: Daniel Kelly, Vice President, NCNB Texas National Bank

• • • • • • • • • • • • • • • • • • • •

Harris and Eliza Kempner Fund
P.O. Box 119
Galveston, TX 77553-0119
(409) 765-6671

Description: Funding for health and medical services, including services for the mentally ill; support for education, welfare, international affairs, human rights, social services, and several other concerns
Restrictions: Giving focused in Galveston, Texas
$ Given: In 1990, 148 grants totaling $997,000 were awarded; average range of $1,000 - $10,000 per award
Application Information: Write for application guidelines; see the important information in the chapter introduction about the need for institutional affiliation.
Deadlines: March 1, August 1, and November 1
Contact: Elaine Perachio, Executive Director

John P. McGovern Foundation
6969 Brompton Street
Houston, TX 77025
(713) 661-4808

Description: Funding for organizations concerned with addiction, family dynamics, and behavioral sciences; support for health agencies and education
Restrictions: Giving focused in the Southwest and Texas, with emphasis on Houston
$ Given: In FY90, 2 grants totaling $2 million were awarded; range of $140 - $2 million per award
Application Information: Most grants initiated by the foundation; unsolicited drug and alcohol addiction funding proposals accepted
Deadline: None
Contact: John P. McGovern, M.D., President

McGovern Fund for the Behavioral Sciences
6969 Brompton Street
Houston, TX 77025
(713) 661-1444

Description: Funding for organizations concerned with addiction, family dynamics, and behavioral sciences; support for health agencies and education
Restrictions: Giving focused in the Southwest and Texas, with emphasis on Houston
$ Given: In FY90, 210 grants totaling $2.1 million were awarded; average range of $1,000 - $10,000 per award
Application Information: Most grants initiated by the foundation; unsolicited drug and alcohol addiction funding proposals accepted
Deadline: None
Contact: John P. McGovern, Chairman and President

J.F. Maddox Foundation

For full description see listing under New Mexico

FLOW-THROUGH FUNDING

· · · · · · · · · · · · · · · · · · ·

**Minnesota Mining and Manu-
facturing Foundation, Inc.**

For full description see listing under Minnesota

**Red River Valley Council
for the Aid of Persons with
Mental Problems, Inc.**
Box 1015
Paris, TX 75460-1015
(214) 785-0351

Description: Funding for equipment for organizations aiding
the intellectually or emotionally handicapped
Restrictions: Giving focused in northeastern Texas and
southeastern Oklahoma
$ Given: In 1989, 8 grants totaling $47,000 were awarded;
range of $2,500 - $10,000 per award
Application Information: Write for application guidelines;
see the important information in the chapter introduction
about the need for institutional affiliation.
Deadline: None
Contact: Dub Basset

**Joseph H. and Florence A.
Roblee Foundation**

For full description see listing under Missouri

The Sonat Foundation

For full description see listing under Alabama

T.L.L. Temple Foundation
109 Temple Boulevard
Lufkin, TX 75901
(409) 639-5197

Description: Funding for health and social services,
including mental health services; support for education,
civic affairs, and culture
Restrictions: Giving focused in the East Texas Pine Timber
Belt counties of Texas
$ Given: In FY90, 132 grants totaling $9.56 million were
awarded; average range of $1,000 - $55,000 per award
Application Information: Write for application guidelines;
see the important information in the chapter introduction
about the need for institutional affiliation.
Deadline: None
Contact: M.F. Buddy Zeagler, Assistant Executive Director
and Controller

• • • • • • • • • • • • • • • • • •

Lola Wright Foundation, Inc.
P.O. Box 1138
Georgetown, TX 78627-1138
(512) 863-5479

Description: Funding for social services, including drug and alcohol abuse programs; support for health services, hospitals, community funds, culture, and several other concerns
Restrictions: Giving strictly limited to Texas, with focus on Austin
$ Given: In 1989, 44 grants totaling $424,500 were awarded; average range of $1,500 - $25,000 per award
Application Information: Write for application guidelines; see the important information in the chapter introduction about the need for institutional affiliation.
Deadlines: February 28 and August 31
Contact: Patrick H. O'Donnell, President

UTAH

Marriner S. Eccles Foundation
701 Deseret Building
79 South Main Street
Salt Lake City, UT 84111
(801) 322-0116

Description: Funding for health and social services, including drug and alcohol abuse programs; support for education, medical research, culture, family services, and disadvantaged populations
Restrictions: Giving strictly limited to Utah
$ Given: In FY90, 83 grants totaling $1.13 million were awarded; average range of $1,000 - $10,000 per award
Application Information: Write for application guidelines; see the important information in the chapter introduction about the need for institutional affiliation.
Deadline: None
Contact: Erma E. Hogan, Manager

Minnesota Mining and Manufacturing Foundation, Inc.

For full description see listing under Minnesota

FLOW-THROUGH FUNDING

. . . .

VIRGINIA

Camp Foundation
P.O. Box 813
Franklin, VA 23851
(804) 562-3439

Description: Funding for local improvements, as well as statewide support for mental illness programs, hospitals, nursing programs, education, safety, culture, and other concerns
Restrictions: Giving focused in Virginia (Franklin, Southampton County, Isle of Wight County, and Tidewater), and northeastern North Carolina
$ Given: In 1990, 53 grants totaling $609,000 were awarded; average range of $1,000 - $20,000 per award
Application Information: Write for application guidelines; see the important information in the chapter introduction about the need for institutional affiliation.
Deadline: Proposals accepted June-August; deadline, September 1
Contact: Harold S. Atkinson, Executive Director

Frederick Foundation, Inc.
3720 Brighton Street
Portsmouth, VA 23707
(804) 393-1605

Description: Funding for health and social services, including substance abuse programs; support for education, religion, and other charitable causes
Restrictions: Giving focused in Hampton Roads, Virginia
$ Given: In 1990, 43 grants totaling $1.14 million were awarded; average range of $1,000 - $175,000 per award
Application Information: Write for application guidelines; see the important information in the chapter introduction about the need for institutional affiliation.
Deadlines: March 15, June 15, September 15, and December 15
Contact: Lawrence W. l'Anson, Jr., President

The Freedom Forum
1101 Wilson Boulevard
Arlington, VA 22209
(703) 528-0800

Description: Funding to support First Amendment freedoms; additional funding for health and social services organizations, including programs for mental health, alcoholism, and drug abuse
Restrictions: Giving focused in areas served by Gannett Company media properties
$ Given: In 1990, 1,162 grants totaling $13.45 million were awarded; average range of $500 - $25,000 per award
Application Information: Proposals from community organizations should be sent to the chief executive of the local Gannett media property (newspaper, broadcast station, advertising office, etc.)
Deadline: None
Contact: Charles L. Overby, President

Little River Foundation
Whitewood Farm
The Plains, VA 22171
(703) 253-5540

Description: Funding for hospitals, drug abuse programs, and AIDS programs; additional support for education, the environment, religion, and community funds
Restrictions: Giving focused in the mid-Atlantic states
$ Given: In FY90, 44 grants totaling $302,000 were awarded; average range of $500 - $100,000 per award
Application Information: Write for application guidelines; see the important information in the chapter introduction about the need for institutional affiliation.
Deadline: None
Contact: Dale D. Hogoboom, Assistant Treasurer

Eugene and Agnes E. Meyer Foundation

For full description see listing under District of Columbia

Minnesota Mining and Manufacturing Foundation, Inc.

For full description see listing under Minnesota

The Norfolk Foundation
1410 Sovran Center
Norfolk, VA 23510
(804) 622-7951

Description: Seed money and special project funding for hospitals, drug abuse programs, mental health programs, education, welfare, and other concerns
Restrictions: Giving focused in Norfolk, Virginia and the area within a 50-mile radius of its boundaries
$ Given: In 1990, 31 grants totaling $1.22 million were awarded; average range of $25,000 - $45,000 per award
Application Information: Write for application guidelines; see the important information in the chapter introduction about the need for institutional affiliation.
Deadline: None
Contact: Lee C. Kitchin, Executive Director

• • • • • • • • • • • • • • • • • • •

**Portsmouth General
Hospital Foundation**
P.O. Box 1053
Portsmouth, VA 23705
(804) 398-4661

Description: General purpose funding for health care, including drug abuse programs
Restrictions: Giving focused in Portsmouth, Virginia
$ Given: In FY91, 31 grants totaling $405,000 were awarded; range of $50 - $102,700 per award
Application Information: Write for application guidelines; see the important information in the chapter introduction about the need for institutional affiliation.
Deadlines: January 31, April 30, July 31, and October 31
Contact: Alan E. Gollihue, Executive Director

**Emerson G. & Dolores G.
Reinsch Foundation**
2040 Columbia Pike
Arlington, VA 22204
(703) 920-3600

Description: Ongoing support for health services, especially programs providing alcoholic rehabilitation and child welfare services
Restrictions: Giving focused in northern Virginia
$ Given: In 1990, 40 grants totaling $75,400 were awarded; range of $20 - $25,000 per award
Application Information: Write for application guidelines; see the important information in the chapter introduction about the need for institutional affiliation.
Deadline: None
Contact: Lola C. Reinsch, Trustee

WASHINGTON

Forest Foundation
820 A Street
Suite 345
Tacoma, WA 98402
(206) 627-1634

Description: Funding for health and social services, including mental health programs; support for Native Americans, the arts, the environment, and other concerns
Restrictions: Giving focused in southwest and western Washington (Pierce County)
$ Given: In FY90, 91 grants totaling $978,000 were awarded; average range of $1,000 - $35,000 per award
Application Information: Write for application guidelines; see the important information in the chapter introduction about the need for institutional affiliation.
Deadline: None
Contact: Frank D. Underwood, Executive Director

Glaser Foundation, Inc.
P.O. Box 6548
Bellevue, WA 98008-0548

Description: Seed money, matching funds, and special project funding for drug abuse programs, health service agencies, youth agencies, and arts organizations
Restrictions: Giving focused in the area of Puget Sound, Washington
$ Given: In FY90, 50 grants totaling $270,500 were awarded; average range of $3,000 - $5,000 per award
Application Information: Write for application guidelines; see the important information in the chapter introduction about the need for institutional affiliation.
Deadline: None
Contact: Joanne Van Sickle

Heileman Old Style Foundation, Inc.

For full description see listing under Wisconsin

The ITT Rayonier Foundation

For full description see listing under Florida

The Samuel S. Johnson Foundation

For full description see listing under Oregon

Minnesota Mining and Manufacturing Foundation, Inc.

For full description see listing under Minnesota

Ray Foundation
1111 Third Avenue
Suite 2770
Seattle, WA 98101
(206) 292-9101

Description: Funding for mental health, drug abuse prevention, scientific research, education, youth agencies, and culture
Restrictions: Giving focused in Arizona, Oregon, and Washington
$ Given: In FY91, 16 grants totaling $411,000 were awarded; range of $1,200 - $150,000 per award
Application Information: Write for application guidelines; see the important information in the chapter introduction about the need for institutional affiliation.
Deadline: None
Contact: Shirley C. Brandenburg, Foundation Administrator

FLOW-THROUGH FUNDING

• • • • • • • • • • • • • • • • • • •

WEST VIRGINIA

**Bernard McDonough
Foundation, Inc.**
1000 Grand Central Mall
P.O. Box 1825
Parkersburg, WV 26102
(304) 485-4494

Description: Funding for health and social service agencies, including drug abuse rehabilitation programs; support for education, civic affairs, culture, etc.
Restrictions: Giving focused in West Virginia; preference for organizations with no other source of funding
$ Given: In 1990, 38 grants totaling $290,000 were awarded; average range of $1,000 - $15,000 per award
Application Information: Write for application guidelines; see the important information in the chapter introduction about the need for institutional affiliation.
Deadline: Proposals accepted in October
Contact: James T. Wakley, President

**Minnesota Mining and Manu-
facturing Foundation, Inc.**

For full description see listing under Minnesota

WISCONSIN

**Briggs & Stratton Corpora-
tion Foundation, Inc.**
12301 West Wirth Street
Wauwatosa, WI 53222
(414) 259-5333
MAILING ADDRESS:
P.O. Box 702, Milwaukee, WI
53201

Description: Funding for alcoholism programs, health, education, rural issues, and other concerns
Restrictions: Giving strictly limited to Wisconsin, with focus on Milwaukee
$ Given: In FY90, 45 grants totaling $429,500 were awarded; average range of $500 - $20,000 per award
Application Information: Write for application guidelines; see the important information in the chapter introduction about the need for institutional affiliation.
Deadline: None
Contact: Kasandra K. Preston, Secretary-Treasurer

• •

Ralph Evinrude Foundation, Inc.
c/o Quarles and Brady
411 East Wisconsin Avenue
Milwaukee, WI 53202-4497
(414) 277-5000

Description: Funding for health agencies, mental health services, hospitals, social services, education, and other concerns
Restrictions: Giving focused in Milwaukee, Wisconsin
$ Given: In FY90, 66 grants totaling $167,400 were awarded; average range of $1,000 - $5,000 per award
Application Information: Write for application guidelines; see the important information in the chapter introduction about the need for institutional affiliation.
Deadlines: Proposals accepted in January, April, July, and October
Contact: Patrick W. Cotter, Vice President

The Evjue Foundation, Inc.
1901 Fish Hatchery Road
P.O. Box 8060
Madison, WI 53708
(608) 252-6401

Description: Funding for mental health, education, social services, youth, and culture
Restrictions: Giving focused in Dane County, Wisconsin
$ Given: In FY90, 122 grants totaling $828,500 were awarded; average range of $1,000 - $5,000 per award
Application Information: Write for application guidelines; see the important information in the chapter introduction about the need for institutional affiliation.
Deadline: Proposals accepted October-November
Contact: Marianne D. Pollard, Executive Secretary

Heileman Old Style Foundation, Inc.
100 Harborview Plaza
P.O. Box 459
LaCrosse, WI 54601
(608) 785-1000

Description: Funding for hospitals, medical research, and alcohol abuse programs; support for education and community funds
Restrictions: Giving focused in the following communities: Perry, GA; Baltimore, MD; Frankenmuth, MI; St. Paul, MN; Portland, OR; Pittsburgh, PA; San Antonio, TX; Seattle, WA; and LaCrosse, WI
$ Given: 120 grants totaling $180,000 were awarded; range of $30 - $2,000 per award
Application Information: Write for application guidelines; see the important information in the chapter introduction about the need for institutional affiliation.
Deadlines: Quarterly
Contact: George E. Smith

The Huffy Foundation, Inc.

For full description see listing under Ohio

FLOW-THROUGH FUNDING

. . . .

Faye McBeath Foundation
1020 North Broadway
Milwaukee, WI 53202
(414) 272-2626

Description: Funding for alcohol and drug abuse programs, as well as for education, housing, health care, welfare, and civic affairs
Restrictions: Giving strictly limited to Wisconsin, with focus on Milwaukee
$ Given: In 1990, grants totaling $1.2 million were awarded; range of $5,000 - $100,000 per award
Application Information: Write for application guidelines; see the important information in the chapter introduction about the need for institutional affiliation.
Deadline: Varies
Contact: Sarah M. Dean, Executive Director

Minnesota Mining and Manufacturing Foundation, Inc.

For full description see listing under Minnesota

The Retirement Research Foundation

For full description see listing under Illinois

Stackner Family Foundation, Inc.
411 East Wisconsin Avenue
Milwaukee, WI 53202-4497
(414) 277-5000

Description: Funding for health agencies, including those serving the mentally ill; support for drug and alcohol abuse programs, education, social services, youth agencies, family services, medical research, and other concerns
Restrictions: Giving focused in Milwaukee, Wisconsin
$ Given: In FY90, 150 grants totaling $1.2 million were awarded; average range of $1,000 - $15,000 per award
Application Information: Write for application guidelines; see the important information in the chapter introduction about the need for institutional affiliation.
Deadlines: March 15, June 15, September 15, and December 15
Contact: Patrick W. Cotter, Executive Director

State and Regional Government Grants

• •

This chapter lists state and regional government agencies that can be of assistance in your search for funding. For the most part, these agencies represent a local level of access to federal funding programs and organizations. For example, the Department of Health and Human Services (DHHS) has several regional offices; individuals or groups applying for funds from a national program must make their applications through their regional offices. Because each government agency administers a number of different funding programs, and because monies that are available vary from year to year, the state-by-state information provided here is, for the most part, listed in generic form. For further details about the federal funding programs administered through these regional offices, please refer to the next chapter, "Federal Grants."

Before you call the contact person in your state, I suggest that you make a list of what it is you need monies for (i.e., hospital bills, medical treatments, long-term care costs). Ask yourself such questions as, are there demonstrated financial needs on the part of the patient or the patient's family? In this fashion, you can address every issue leading to support and aid in one telephone call — by being able to describe precisely the kinds of funding for which you may be eligible.

When you call, ask, "What kinds of funding programs do you provide? Can I apply directly as an individual or do I need to apply through a local agency, and if so, can you

•   •

direct me to the appropriate agency?" If the agency you call does not offer a program to meet your particular needs, someone there may be able to direct you to an agency that does. If the agency publishes materials describing its funding programs, request that these be mailed to you, along with an application. Also make sure to find out if there is a deadline coming up so that you will be able to return any applications by that time.

• •

ALABAMA

Federal Emergency Management Agency, Region IV Office
1371 Peachtree Street, N.E.
Suite 700
Atlanta, GA 30309-3108
(404) 853-4200

Programs: See the Federal Grants chapter for the following listing:
• Mental Health Disaster Assistance and Emergency Mental Health
Contact: Major P. May, Regional Director

ALASKA

Federal Emergency Management Agency, Region X Office
Federal Regional Center
130-228th Street, S.W.
Bothell, WA 98021-9796
(206) 487-4604

Programs: See the Federal Grants chapter for the following listing:
• Mental Health Disaster Assistance and Emergency Mental Health
Contact: Mr. Kim Whitman, Regional Director

ARIZONA

Federal Emergency Management Agency, Region IX Office
Presidio of San Francisco
Building 105
San Francisco, CA 94129-1250
(415) 923-7100

Programs: See the Federal Grants chapter for the following listing:
• Mental Health Disaster Assistance and Emergency Mental Health
Contact: William Medigovich, Regional Director

ARKANSAS

Federal Emergency Management Agency, Region VI Office
Federal Regional Center
Room 206-800
North Loop 288
Denton, TX 76201-3698
(817) 898-5104

Programs: See the Federal Grants chapter for the following listing:
• Mental Health Disaster Assistance and Emergency Mental Health
Contact: Bradley M. Harris, Regional Director

STATE AND REGIONAL GOVERNMENT GRANTS

. . . .

CALIFORNIA

Federal Emergency Management Agency, Region IX Office
Presidio of San Francisco
Building 105
San Francisco, CA 94129-1250
(415) 923-7100

Programs: See the Federal Grants chapter for the following listing:
• Mental Health Disaster Assistance and Emergency Mental Health
Contact: William Medigovich, Regional Director

COLORADO

Federal Emergency Management Agency, Region VIII Office
Denver Federal Center
Building 710, Box 25267
Denver, CO 80225-0267
(303) 235-4812

Programs: See the Federal Grants chapter for the following listing:
• Mental Health Disaster Assistance and Emergency Mental Health
Contact: Marian L. Olson, Regional Director

CONNECTICUT

Federal Emergency Management Agency, Region I Office
J.W. McCormack Post Office
& Courthouse Building
Room 442
Boston, MA 02109-4595
(617) 223-9540

Programs: See the Federal Grants chapter for the following listing:
• Mental Health Disaster Assistance and Emergency Mental Health
Contact: Richard H. Strome, Regional Director

DELAWARE

Federal Emergency Management Agency, Region III Office
Liberty Square Bldg., 2nd Fl.
105 South Seventh Street
Philadelphia, PA 19106-3316
(215) 931-5608

Programs: See the Federal Grants chapter for the following listing:
• Mental Health Disaster Assistance and Emergency Mental Health
Contact: Paul P. Giordano, Regional Director

• •

DISTRICT OF COLUMBIA

Federal Emergency Management Agency, Region III Office
Liberty Square Building
2nd Floor
105 South Seventh Street
Philadelphia, PA 19106-3316
(215) 931-5608

Programs: See the Federal Grants chapter for the following listing:
• Mental Health Disaster Assistance and Emergency Mental Health
Contact: Paul P. Giordano, Regional Director

FLORIDA

Federal Emergency Management Agency, Region IV Office
1371 Peachtree Street, N.E.
Suite 700
Atlanta, GA 30309-3108
(404) 853-4200

Programs: See the Federal Grants chapter for the following listing:
• Mental Health Disaster Assistance and Emergency Mental Health
Contact: Major P. May, Regional Director

GEORGIA

Federal Emergency Management Agency, Region IV Office
1371 Peachtree Street, N.E.
Suite 700
Atlanta, GA 30309-3108
(404) 853-4200

Programs: See the Federal Grants chapter for the following listing:
• Mental Health Disaster Assistance and Emergency Mental Health
Contact: Major P. May, Regional Director

HAWAII

Federal Emergency Management Agency, Region IX Office
Presidio of San Francisco
Building 105
San Francisco, CA 94129-1250
(415) 923-7100

Programs: See the Federal Grants chapter for the following listing:
• Mental Health Disaster Assistance and Emergency Mental Health
Contact: William Medigovich, Regional Director

STATE AND REGIONAL GOVERNMENT GRANTS

• •

IDAHO

**Federal Emergency
Management Agency,
Region X Office**
Federal Regional Center
130-228th Street, S.W.
Bothell, WA 98021-9796
(206) 487-4604

Programs: See the Federal Grants chapter for the following listing:
• Mental Health Disaster Assistance and Emergency Mental Health
Contact: Mr. Kim Whitman, Regional Director

ILLINOIS

**Federal Emergency
Management Agency,
Region V Office**
175 West Jackson Boulevard
4th Floor
Chicago, IL 60604-2698
(312) 408-5501

Programs: See the Federal Grants chapter for the following listing:
• Mental Health Disaster Assistance and Emergency Mental Health
Contact: Mr. Arlyn F. Brower, Regional Director

INDIANA

**Federal Emergency
Management Agency,
Region V Office**
175 West Jackson Boulevard
4th Floor
Chicago, IL 60604-2698
(312) 408-5501

Programs: See the Federal Grants chapter for the following listing:
• Mental Health Disaster Assistance and Emergency Mental Health
Contact: Mr. Arlyn F. Brower, Regional Director

IOWA

**Federal Emergency
Management Agency,
Region VII Office**
911 Walnut Street
Room 200
Kansas City, MO 64106-2085
(816) 283-7061

Programs: See the Federal Grants chapter for the following listing:
• Mental Health Disaster Assistance and Emergency Mental Health
Contact: Mr. S. Richard Mellinger, Regional Director

. . . .

KANSAS

Federal Emergency Management Agency, Region VII Office
911 Walnut Street
Room 200
Kansas City, MO 64106-2085
(816) 283-7061

Programs: See the Federal Grants chapter for the following listing:
• Mental Health Disaster Assistance and Emergency Mental Health
Contact: Mr. S. Richard Mellinger, Regional Director

KENTUCKY

Federal Emergency Management Agency, Region IV Office
1371 Peachtree Street, N.E.
Suite 700
Atlanta, GA 30309-3108
(404) 853-4200

Programs: See the Federal Grants chapter for the following listing:
• Mental Health Disaster Assistance and Emergency Mental Health
Contact: Major P. May, Regional Director

LOUISIANA

Federal Emergency Management Agency, Region VI Office
Federal Regional Center
Room 206-800
North Loop 288
Denton, TX 76201-3698
(817) 898-5104

Programs: See the Federal Grants chapter for the following listing:
• Mental Health Disaster Assistance and Emergency Mental Health
Contact: Bradley M. Harris, Regional Director

MAINE

Federal Emergency Management Agency, Region I Office
J.W. McCormack Post Office
& Courthouse Building
Room 442
Boston, MA 02109-4595
(617) 223-9540

Programs: See the Federal Grants chapter for the following listing:
• Mental Health Disaster Assistance and Emergency Mental Health
Contact: Richard H. Strome, Regional Director

STATE AND REGIONAL GOVERNMENT GRANTS

• • • • • • • • • • • • • • • • • • •

MARYLAND

Federal Emergency Management Agency, Region III Office
Liberty Square Bldg., 2nd Fl.
105 South Seventh Street
Philadelphia, PA 19106-3316
(215) 931-5608

Programs: See the Federal Grants chapter for the following listing:
• Mental Health Disaster Assistance and Emergency Mental Health
Contact: Paul P. Giordano, Regional Director

MASSACHUSETTS

Federal Emergency Management Agency, Region I Office
J.W. McCormack Post Office
& Courthouse Bldg., Rm. 442
Boston, MA 02109-4595
(617) 223-9540

Programs: See the Federal Grants chapter for the following listing:
• Mental Health Disaster Assistance and Emergency Mental Health
Contact: Richard H. Strome, Regional Director

MICHIGAN

Federal Emergency Management Agency, Region V Office
175 West Jackson Boulevard
4th Floor
Chicago, IL 60604-2698
(312) 408-5501

Programs: See the Federal Grants chapter for the following listing:
• Mental Health Disaster Assistance and Emergency Mental Health
Contact: Mr. Arlyn F. Brower, Regional Director

MINNESOTA

Federal Emergency Management Agency, Region V Office
175 West Jackson Boulevard
4th Floor
Chicago, IL 60604-2698
(312) 408-5501

Programs: See the Federal Grants chapter for the following listing:
• Mental Health Disaster Assistance and Emergency Mental Health
Contact: Mr. Arlyn F. Brower, Regional Director

• • • • • • • • • • • • • • • • • • • •

MISSISSIPPI

Federal Emergency Management Agency, Region IV Office
1371 Peachtree Street, N.E.
Suite 700
Atlanta, GA 30309-3108
(404) 853-4200

Programs: See the Federal Grants chapter for the following listing:
• Mental Health Disaster Assistance and Emergency Mental Health
Contact: Major P. May, Regional Director

MISSOURI

Federal Emergency Management Agency, Region VII Office
911 Walnut Street, Rm. 200
Kansas City, MO 64106-2085
(816) 283-7061

Programs: See the Federal Grants chapter for the following listing:
• Mental Health Disaster Assistance and Emergency Mental Health
Contact: Mr. S. Richard Mellinger, Regional Director

MONTANA

Federal Emergency Management Agency, Region VIII Office
Denver Federal Center
Building 710
Box 25267
Denver, CO 80225-0267
(303) 235-4812

Programs: See the Federal Grants chapter for the following listing:
• Mental Health Disaster Assistance and Emergency Mental Health
Contact: Marian L. Olson, Regional Director

NEBRASKA

Federal Emergency Management Agency, Region VII Office
911 Walnut Street
Room 200
Kansas City, MO 64106-2085
(816) 283-7061

Programs: See the Federal Grants chapter for the following listing:
• Mental Health Disaster Assistance and Emergency Mental Health
Contact: Mr. S. Richard Mellinger, Regional Director

STATE AND REGIONAL GOVERNMENT GRANTS

• • • • • • • • • • • • • • • • • • • •

NEVADA

Federal Emergency Management Agency, Region IX Office
Presidio of San Francisco
Building 105
San Francisco, CA 94129-1250
(415) 923-7100

Programs: See the Federal Grants chapter for the following listing:
• Mental Health Disaster Assistance and Emergency Mental Health
Contact: William Medigovich, Regional Director

NEW HAMPSHIRE

Federal Emergency Management Agency, Region I Office
J.W. McCormack Post Office
& Courthouse Building
Room 442
Boston, MA 02109-4595
(617) 223-9540

Programs: See the Federal Grants chapter for the following listing:
• Mental Health Disaster Assistance and Emergency Mental Health
Contact: Richard H. Strome, Regional Director

NEW JERSEY

Federal Emergency Management Agency, Region II Office
26 Federal Plaza, Room 1337
New York, NY 10278-0002
(212) 225-7209

Programs: See the Federal Grants chapter for the following listing:
• Mental Health Disaster Assistance and Emergency Mental Health
Contact: Stephen Kempf, Jr., Regional Director

NEW MEXICO

Federal Emergency Management Agency, Region VI Office
Federal Regional Center
Room 206-800
North Loop 288
Denton, TX 76201-3698
(817) 898-5104

Programs: See the Federal Grants chapter for the following listing:
• Mental Health Disaster Assistance and Emergency Mental Health
Contact: Bradley M. Harris, Regional Director

. . . .

NEW YORK

**Federal Emergency
Management Agency,
Region II Office**
26 Federal Plaza, Room 1337
New York, NY 10278-0002
(212) 225-7209

Programs: See the Federal Grants chapter for the following listing:
• Mental Health Disaster Assistance and Emergency Mental Health
Contact: Stephen Kempf, Jr., Regional Director

NORTH CAROLINA

**Federal Emergency
Management Agency,
Region IV Office**
1371 Peachtree Street, N.E.
Suite 700
Atlanta, GA 30309-3108
(404) 853-4200

Programs: See the Federal Grants chapter for the following listing:
• Mental Health Disaster Assistance and Emergency Mental Health
Contact: Major P. May, Regional Director

NORTH DAKOTA

**Federal Emergency
Management Agency,
Region VIII Office**
Denver Federal Center
Building 710
Box 25267
Denver, CO 80225-0267
(303) 235-4812

Programs: See the Federal Grants chapter for the following listing:
• Mental Health Disaster Assistance and Emergency Mental Health
Contact: Marian L. Olson, Regional Director

OHIO

**Federal Emergency
Management Agency,
Region V Office**
175 West Jackson Boulevard
4th Floor
Chicago, IL 60604-2698
(312) 408-5501

Programs: See the Federal Grants chapter for the following listing:
• Mental Health Disaster Assistance and Emergency Mental Health
Contact: Mr. Arlyn F. Brower, Regional Director

STATE AND REGIONAL GOVERNMENT GRANTS

• •

OKLAHOMA

Federal Emergency Management Agency, Region VI Office
Federal Regional Center
Room 206-800
North Loop 288
Denton, TX 76201-3698
(817) 898-5104

Programs: See the Federal Grants chapter for the following listing:
• Mental Health Disaster Assistance and Emergency Mental Health
Contact: Bradley M. Harris, Regional Director

OREGON

Federal Emergency Management Agency, Region X Office
Federal Regional Center
130-228th Street, S.W.
Bothell, WA 98021-9796
(206) 487-4604

Programs: See the Federal Grants chapter for the following listing:
• Mental Health Disaster Assistance and Emergency Mental Health
Contact: Mr. Kim Whitman, Regional Director

PENNSYLVANIA

Federal Emergency Management Agency, Region III Office
Liberty Square Bldg., 2nd Fl.
105 South Seventh Street
Philadelphia, PA 19106-3316
(215) 931-5608

Programs: See the Federal Grants chapter for the following listing:
• Mental Health Disaster Assistance and Emergency Mental Health
Contact: Paul P. Giordano, Regional Director

PUERTO RICO

Federal Emergency Management Agency, Region II Office
26 Federal Plaza
Room 1337
New York, NY 10278-0002
(212) 225-7209

Programs: See the Federal Grants chapter for the following listing:
• Mental Health Disaster Assistance and Emergency Mental Health
Contact: Stephen Kempf, Jr., Regional Director

RHODE ISLAND

**Federal Emergency
Management Agency,
Region I Office**
J.W. McCormack Post Office
& Courthouse Bldg., Rm. 442
Boston, MA 02109-4595
(617) 223-9540

Programs: See the Federal Grants chapter for the following
listing:
• Mental Health Disaster Assistance and Emergency Mental
Health
Contact: Richard H. Strome, Regional Director

SOUTH CAROLINA

**Federal Emergency
Management Agency,
Region IV Office**
1371 Peachtree Street, N.E.
Suite 700
Atlanta, GA 30309-3108
(404) 853-4200

Programs: See the Federal Grants chapter for the following
listing:
• Mental Health Disaster Assistance and Emergency Mental
Health
Contact: Major P. May, Regional Director

SOUTH DAKOTA

**Federal Emergency
Management Agency,
Region VIII Office**
Denver Federal Center
Building 710, Box 25267
Denver, CO 80225-0267
(303) 235-4812

Programs: See the Federal Grants chapter for the following
listing:
• Mental Health Disaster Assistance and Emergency Mental
Health
Contact: Marian L. Olson, Regional Director

TENNESSEE

**Federal Emergency
Management Agency,
Region IV Office**
1371 Peachtree Street, N.E.
Suite 700
Atlanta, GA 30309-3108
(404) 853-4200

Programs: See the Federal Grants chapter for the following
listing:
• Mental Health Disaster Assistance and Emergency Mental
Health
Contact: Major P. May, Regional Director

STATE AND REGIONAL GOVERNMENT GRANTS

. . . .

TEXAS

Federal Emergency Management Agency, Region VI Office
Federal Regional Center
Rm. 206-800, North Loop 288
Denton, TX 76201-3698
(817) 898-5104

Programs: See the Federal Grants chapter for the following listing:
• Mental Health Disaster Assistance and Emergency Mental Health
Contact: Bradley M. Harris, Regional Director

U.S. VIRGIN ISLANDS

Federal Emergency Management Agency, Region II Office
26 Federal Plaza, Room 1337
New York, NY 10278-0002
(212) 225-7209

Programs: See the Federal Grants chapter for the following listing:
• Mental Health Disaster Assistance and Emergency Mental Health
Contact: Stephen Kempf, Jr., Regional Director

UTAH

Federal Emergency Management Agency, Region VIII Office
Denver Federal Center
Building 710
Box 25267
Denver, CO 80225-0267
(303) 235-4812

Programs: See the Federal Grants chapter for the following listing:
• Mental Health Disaster Assistance and Emergency Mental Health
Contact: Marian L. Olson, Regional Director

VERMONT

Federal Emergency Management Agency, Region I Office
J.W. McCormack Post Office
& Courthouse Building
Room 442
Boston, MA 02109-4595
(617) 223-9540

Programs: See the Federal Grants chapter for the following listing:
• Mental Health Disaster Assistance and Emergency Mental Health
Contact: Richard H. Strome, Regional Director

. . . .

VIRGINIA

Federal Emergency Management Agency, Region III Office
Liberty Square Bldg., 2nd Fl.
105 South Seventh Street
Philadelphia, PA 19106-3316
(215) 931-5608

Programs: See the Federal Grants chapter for the following listing:
• Mental Health Disaster Assistance and Emergency Mental Health
Contact: Paul P. Giordano, Regional Director

WASHINGTON

Federal Emergency Management Agency, Region X Office
Federal Regional Center
130-228th Street, S.W.
Bothell, WA 98021-9796
(206) 487-4604

Programs: See the Federal Grants chapter for the following listing:
• Mental Health Disaster Assistance and Emergency Mental Health
Contact: Mr. Kim Whitman, Regional Director

WEST VIRGINIA

Federal Emergency Management Agency, Region III Office
Liberty Square Bldg., 2nd Fl.
105 South Seventh Street
Philadelphia, PA 19106-3316
(215) 931-5608

Programs: See the Federal Grants chapter for the following listing:
• Mental Health Disaster Assistance and Emergency Mental Health
Contact: Paul P. Giordano, Regional Director

WISCONSIN

Federal Emergency Management Agency, Region V Office
175 West Jackson Boulevard
4th Floor
Chicago, IL 60604-2698
(312) 408-5501

Programs: See the Federal Grants chapter for the following listing:
• Mental Health Disaster Assistance and Emergency Mental Health
Contact: Mr. Arlyn F. Brower, Regional Director

STATE AND REGIONAL GOVERNMENT GRANTS

. . . .

WYOMING

**Federal Emergency
Management Agency,
Region VIII Office**
Denver Federal Center
Building 710
Box 25267
Denver, CO 80225-0267
(303) 235-4812

Programs: See the Federal Grants chapter for the following listing:
• Mental Health Disaster Assistance and Emergency Mental Health
Contact: Marian L. Olson, Regional Director

Federal Grants

. . . .

The following chapter includes a limited number of health-related financial assistance programs funded by the federal government. Some of these listings are detailed descriptions of federal programs administered through the regional offices listed in the previous chapter. If one of these programs seems appropriate for your funding needs, please refer back to the previous chapter, "State and Regional Government Grants," for the address of your local office.

Remember, federal grant sources are not always as narrowly defined in purpose or as accessible to individuals as private sector funders. Often, however, the dollar amounts are larger and worth the trouble.

Before you call the contact person in your state, I suggest that you make a list of what it is you need monies for (i.e., hospital bills, medical treatments, long-term care costs). Ask yourself such questions as, are there demonstrated financial needs on the part of the patient or the patient's family? In this fashion, you can address every issue leading to support and aid in one telephone call — by being able to describe precisely the kinds of funding for which you may be eligible.

When you call, ask, "What kinds of funding programs do you provide? Can I apply directly as an individual or do I need to apply through a local agency, and if so, can you direct me to the appropriate agency?" If the agency

· · · · · · · · · · · · · · · · · · ·

you call does not offer a program to meet your particular
needs, someone there may be able to direct you to an
agency that does. If the agency publishes materials
describing its funding programs, request that these be
mailed to you, along with an application. Also make sure
to find out if there is a deadline coming up so that you
will be able to return any applications by that time.

. . . .

ALCOHOL AND DRUG ABUSE
and
MENTAL HEALTH SERVICES BLOCK GRANT

PROGRAM HEADQUARTERS
Block Grant Programs
Office for Treatment Improvement
Alcohol, Drug Abuse and Mental Health Administration
Public Health Service
Department of Health and Human Services
10th Floor
Rockwall II Building
5600 Fishers Lane
Rockville, MD 20857
(301) 443-3820
Contact: Sue Becker, Director

and

GRANTS MANAGEMENT
Block Grant Programs
Division of Grants and Contracts Management
Alcohol, Drug Abuse and Mental Health Administration
Public Health Service
Department of Health and Human Services
Room 13C-20
Parklawn Building
5600 Fishers Lane
Rockville, MD 20857
(301) 443-3334
Contact: Thomas M. Reynolds, Grants Management Officer

Program: Alcohol and Drug Abuse and Mental Health Services Block Grant (Federal program 93.992)
Description: Formula grants for support of community mental health care centers, for provision of mental health care services to the chronically mentally ill, for coordination of mental health and medical health care services, and for improved treatment/rehabilitation programs for substance abusers
Restrictions: State governments, Indian tribes, and tribal organizations may apply for funds
$ Given: $54,000 to $140 million per award; average award, $20.2 million
Number of Awards: Approximately 60 block grants are awarded annually
Application Information: Eligible government/tribal organizations must apply annually for allotment of funds
Contact: Individuals requesting services contact state agencies providing mental health care services

FEDERAL GRANTS

• • • • • • • • • • • • • • • • • • • •

MENTAL HEALTH DISASTER ASSISTANCE
and
EMERGENCY MENTAL HEALTH

PROGRAM HEADQUARTERS
National Institute of Mental Health
Alcohol, Drug Abuse and Mental Health Administration
Public Health Service
Department of Health and Human Services
Room 18-105
Parklawn Building
5600 Fishers Lane
Rockville, MD 20857
(301) 443-4735
Contact: Dr. Brian Flynn, Emergency Services Coordinator

and

GRANTS MANAGEMENT
National Institute of Mental Health
Alcohol, Drug Abuse and Mental Health Administration
Public Health Service
Department of Health and Human Services
Room 7C-15
Parklawn Building
5600 Fishers Lane
Rockville, MD 20857
(301) 443-3065
Contact: Bruce Ringler, Grants Management Officer

Program: Mental Health Disaster Assistance and Emergency Mental Health (Federal program 93.982)
Description: Project grants for provision of emergency mental health counseling to people affected by major disasters; funding for training of volunteers to provide counseling; no funding for long-term treatment
Restrictions: State and local government agencies (if recommended by the Governor and approved by the Secretary) may apply for funds
$ Given: $14,500 to $1.5 million per award; average award, $420,000
Number of Awards: Awards are made on a case-by-case basis, contingent upon occurrence of disasters and emergencies
Application Information: Individuals seeking mental health counseling following a major disaster should contact their regional offices of the Federal Emergency Management Agency **(see previous chapter)**

. . . .

MENTAL HEALTH PLANNING AND DEMONSTRATION PROJECTS

PROGRAM HEADQUARTERS
Community Section
Systems Development and Community Support Branch
Division of Applied and Services Research
National Institute of Mental Health
Alcohol, Drug Abuse and Mental Health Administration
Public Health Service
Department of Health and Human Services
Room 11C-22
Parklawn Building
5600 Fishers Lane
Rockville, MD 20857
(301) 443-3653
Contact: Neal Brown, Chief

and

GRANTS MANAGEMENT
National Institute of Mental Health
Alcohol, Drug Abuse and Mental Health Administration
Public Health Service
Department of Health and Human Services
Room 7C-15
Parklawn Building
5600 Fishers Lane
Rockville, MD 20857
(301) 443-3065
Contact: Bruce Ringler, Grants Management Officer

Program: Mental Health Planning and Demonstration Projects (Federal program 93.125)
Description: Project grants to develop community support systems for individuals with chronic mental illnesses and to improve the delivery of mental health services to the same populations
Restrictions: Only state mental health authorities may apply for funding
$ Given: $10,000 to $1.66 million per award; average award, $212,000
Number of Awards: Approximately 125-150 projects are funded annually
Application Information: Interested individuals should contact state mental health authorities for information

FEDERAL GRANTS

. . . .

PROTECTION AND ADVOCACY FOR MENTALLY ILL INDIVIDUALS

PROGRAM HEADQUARTERS
Division of Applied and Services Research
National Institute of Mental Health
Alcohol, Drug Abuse and Mental Health Administration
Public Health Service
Department of Health and Human Services
Room 18C-26
Parklawn Building
5600 Fishers Lane
Rockville, MD 20857
(301) 443-3606
Contact: Dr. Samuel Keith, Acting Director

and

GRANTS MANAGEMENT
National Institute of Mental Health
Alcohol, Drug Abuse and Mental Health Administration
Public Health Service
Department of Health and Human Services
Room 7C-15
Parklawn Building
5600 Fishers Lane
Rockville, MD 20857
(301) 443-3065
Contact: Bruce Ringler, Grants Management Officer

Program: Protection and Advocacy for Mentally Ill Individuals (Federal program 93.138)
Description: Formula grants for the establishment of protection and advocacy services for the mentally ill; program activities seek to protect the rights of mentally ill individuals and to investigate and redress reported incidents of neglect
Restrictions: State and local government agencies, as well as designated public and private advocacy organizations, may apply for funding
$ Given: $100,000 to $1.3 million per award; average award, $273,000; funding provided to all states and territories
Application Information: A mentally ill individual who wants to request advocacy services must meet the following eligibility requirements: (1) be an inpatient or resident in a mental health care facility; or (2) have been discharged from such a facility within the past 90 days

• •

VETERANS HOSPITALIZATION

Director, Administrative Services
Department of Veterans Affairs
Washington, DC 20420
(202) 535-7384

Program: Veterans Hospitalization (Federal program 64.009)
Description: Inpatient medical, surgical, and neuropsychiatric care for eligible veterans; includes mental health services and professional counseling, as appropriate
Restrictions: Benefits available to any veteran who (1) requires treatment for a service-connected disability or disease, or (2) has a service-connected disability but is in need of treatment for a nonservice-connected condition, or (3) has been honorably discharged and meets minimum active duty requirements, or (4) receives a VA pension, or is a former POW; benefits are also available to the spouse or child of a veteran with total, permanent disability resulting from a service-connected disability, as well as to the widow, widower, or child of a person who died on active duty; Medicare and CHAMPUS eligibility may interfere with VA benefits; nonservice disabled veterans with incomes above certain levels may be treated on a resource-available basis and must agree to pay applicable co-payments
$ Given: Services provided; approximately $7.5 billion is allotted annually nationwide for services provided through this program
Application Information: Eligible persons may apply personally at a VA Medical Center, through any veterans service organization representative, or by mailing VA Form 10-10 to the nearest VA health care facility
Contact: Local VA Medical Center

VETERANS OUTPATIENT CARE

Director, Administrative Services
Department of Veterans Affairs
Washington, DC 20420
(202) 535-7384

Program: Veterans Outpatient Care (Federal program 64.011)
Description: Medical and dental services, medicines, and medical supplies for eligible veterans provided on an outpatient basis; includes readjustment counseling for Vietnam era veterans, provided at VA facilities or at outreach centers
Restrictions: Eligibility requirements are similar but not identical to those for Veterans Hospitalization (Federal program 64.009); check with local Veterans Administration for details
$ Given: Services and goods provided; approximately $3 - $3.5 billion is allotted annually nationwide for this program
Contact: Local VA Medical Center

Index

X

Y

Z

Books in Laurie Blum's **Free Money** Series

• • • • • • • • • • • • • • • • • • •

THE FREE MONEY FOR CHILD CARE SERIES

Free Money for Day Care
• Advice on finding financial aid for family day care, child care centers, in-house care, and camp and summer programs

Free Money for Private Schools
• Where to find money for preschool and nursery education, private primary schools, and private secondary schools

Free Money for Children's Medical and Dental Care
• Ways to receive money for both long- and short-term medical care, dental and orthodontic treatment, and dermatological procedures

Free Money for Behavioral and Genetic Childhood Disorders
• Free Money for treatment of learning disabilities, eating disorders, retardation, alcohol and drug abuse, neurological disturbances, and sleep disorders

THE FREE MONEY FOR HEALTH CARE SERIES

Free Money for Diseases of Aging
• Find money to help pay for major surgery and medical care for diseases of aging such as Alzheimer's, Parkinson's, stroke, and other chronic illnesses

Free Money for Heart Disease and Cancer Care
• Ways to receive money for the diagnosis and treatment (surgery or long-term care) of cancer and heart disease

Free Money for Fertility Treatments
• Where to look for Free Money for infertility testing, treatment, insemination, and preliminary adoption expenses

Free Money for the Care and Treatment of Mental and Emotional Disorders
• Detailed guidance on locating Free Money for psychological care

WITHDRAWN
No longer the property of the
Boston Public Library.
Sale of this material benefits the Library